I0201790

101
Prayers in the Bible

Biblical Lessons
and Bible Scriptures

Compiled by Akili Kumasi

GIL PUBLICATIONS
THE GOD IS LOVE MINISTRIES
P. O. Box 80275, Brooklyn, NY 11208
www.GILpublications.com

101 Prayers in the Bible
Biblical Lessons and Bible Scriptures

Compiled by Akili Kumasi

ISBN-10: 0-9626035-7-0
ISBN-13: 978-0-9626035-7-0
Copyright © 2007 by GIL Publications
A division of The God Is Love Ministries

Scriptures marked (KJV) are taken from the King James Version of the Bible.

Scriptures marked (NIV) are taken from the New International Version of the Bible Scripture taken from the Holy Bible, NEW INTERNATIONAL VERSION®. Copyright © 1973, 1978, 1984 International Bible Society. All rights reserved throughout the world. Used by permission of International Bible Society. NEW INTERNATIONAL VERSION® and NIV® are registered trademarks of International Bible Society. Use of either trademark for the offering of goods or services requires the prior written consent of International Bible Society.

Versus marked (TLB) are taken from The Living Bible, copyright © 1971. Used by permission of Tyndale House Publishers, Inc., Wheaton Illinois 60189. All rights reserved.

Scripture quotations marked (NLT) are taken from the Holy Bible, New Living Translation, copyright © 1996. Used by permission of Tyndale House Publishers, Inc., Wheaton, Illinois 60189. All rights reserved.

Scripture marked NASB® are taken from the New American Standard Bible®. "Scripture quotations taken from the New American Standard Bible®, Copyright © 1960, 1962, 1963, 1968, 1971, 1972, 1973, 1975, 1977, 1995 by The Lockman Foundation. Used by permission." (www.Lockman.org)

Scripture marked AMP® are taken from the Amplified® Bible. Scripture quotations taken from the Amplified® Bible, Copyright © 1954, 1958, 1962, 1964, 1965, 1987 by The Lockman Foundation. Used by permission." (www.Lockman.org)

Scriptures marked as "(CEV)" are taken from the Contemporary English Version Copyright © 1995 by American Bible Society. Used by permission.

The Cover Art is by ChristArt.com

GIL PUBLICATIONS
THE GOD IS LOVE MINISTRIES
P. O. Box 80275, Brooklyn, NY 11208
orders@GILpublications.com
www.GILpublications.com

101
Prayers in the Bible
Biblical Lessons and Bible Scriptures

Table of Contents

Introduction

While compiling the scriptures for this book and writing the Bible Study Article on the Power of Prayer, I have had one of the greatest experiences in my life in the presence of the Lord.

God has shown me wonderful things about who He is and the importance of prayer in my life. Make no mistake about it, without prayer we cannot hope to be successful in anything that we do. But with prayer, God is on our side and we get on His side.

Part of this experience had been the rediscovery of the following hymn that sums it all up for me.

What a Friend We Have In Jesus[1]

What a Friend we have in Jesus,
    All our sins and griefs to bear!
What a privilege to carry
    Everything to God in prayer!
O what peace we often forfeit,
    O what needless pain we bear,
All because we do not carry
    Everything to God in prayer!

Have we trials and temptations?
    Is there trouble anywhere?
We should never be discouraged;
    Take it to the Lord in prayer!
Can we find a friend so faithful
    Who will all our sorrows share?
Jesus knows our every weakness;
    Take it to the Lord in prayer!

---

[1] *What a Friend We have In Jesus*, Lyrics: Joseph Scriven, 1855. Composer: Charles Converse, 1868. Copied from http://www.biblestudycharts.com.

Are we weak and heavy laden,
   Cumbered with a load of care?
Precious Savior, still our Refuge
   Take it to the Lord in prayer!
Do thy friends despise, forsake thee?
   Take it to the Lord in prayer!
In His arms He'll take and shield thee,
   Thou wilt find a solace there.

For a great website that has the lyrics (and the music you can listen to) to over 500 hymns, including many especially for children please see www.biblestudycharts.com.

I pray that you too will be blessed by this book of scriptures on prayer.

Akili Kumasi

The
Power of Prayer

Is There Power in Prayer?

By Akili Kumasi

God revealed to me one day that there is no real power in our prayers because real POWER IS ONLY IN HIM.

Now, I'm sure that some of you will look at the first part of that statement and question if it is un-Biblical non-sense. But, I assure you, that it is very Biblically accurate.

But, please – do not take my word for anything. Please examine every scripture that is used in this Bible Study Article and scrutinize every statement to see if it lines up with Biblical truth. This is how God says we should accept any Biblical message that is presented (Acts 17:10-12).

You might have heard the statement many, many times that *"there is power in prayer."*

In fact, one of the Pastors at my church often says, *"No prayer, no power. Little prayer, little power. Much prayer, much power."*

One could think that the opening statement flies in the face of wisdom from James 5:16. Let us look at this verse in the New International Version of the Bible (NIV):

The prayer of a righteous man is powerful and effective.
James 5:15 NIV

Now, the New Living Translation (NLT):

The earnest prayer of a righteous person has great power and wonderful results.
James 5:16 NLT

So what does it mean to say that there is no real power in prayer?

What is Real Power?

Real power (in this instance) is the power to "answer" prayers. This power is not contained in the prayer (in and of itself). Nor is it with the person who is praying.

The power to answer prayers rests solely with God. This might seem very simplistic. However, as you read this Bible Study Article you will hopefully see why this point is very important, and also, how to experience God's power in your life.

There are four main types of power broadly discussed in the New Testament of the Bible. To understand their separate and distinct meanings we used the *Strong's Concordance*[2] to examine the Greek words that were used in the original writings.

1) **kratos** (#G2904) which means "mighty, great power, dominion" - This word is used to refer to the power and sovereignty of God.

2) **exousia** (#G1849) which means "power of authority or position" - This word is used when referring to the authority that God delegated to us (Saved Christians).

---

[2] If you do not have access to the *Strong's Concordance* see our website (www.gilpublications.com) for links to Bible search websites that have many Bible translations (versions), concordances, dictionaries and lexicons which can be very helpful Bible study tools.

3) **dynamis** (#G1411) which means "strength, power, ability inherent or residing in a thing" - This word refers to strength or power of a person or thing.

4) **ischus** (#G2479) which means "forcefulness (literally or figuratively)" - This word refers to the exercise of force or how forceful something is.

Now let us look at our main scripture, James 5:16, from the King James Version of the Bible:

> **The effectual fervent prayer of a righteous man availeth much.**
>
> James 5:16 KJV

The word **availeth**[3] comes from the Greek word **ischou** (#G2480), which means "to have (or exercise) force." **Ischou** comes from the fourth **power** word above, **ischus** (#G2479) which means "forcefulness."

Ischou (or **availeth**) is not the power to answer prayers. It means to exert "force" or to "push" to make something happen. If we substitute the meaning of the word "**availeth/ischou**" into the scripture we get this: The effectual fervent prayer of a righteous man "exerts much force." I have heard preached on more than one occasion: PUSH – Pray Until Something Happens. This is what God wants us to do. He wants us to push (through prayer) to make something happen.

God also wants to remind His people that prayer is not a performance or a magical chant that produces results at will. Prayer is a petition to God, a request. Prayer is communication with God and a mighty weapon if employed properly.

---

[3] Quoted scriptures are in bold (without italics).

God wants us to focus on Him, His power as the creator, provider and sustainer of the universe. He is the center of all things. And remember, our God is a loving God (John 3:16; 1 John 4). He wants to give us the kingdom (Luke 12:32). He wants to answer our prayers. That is why He has given us so many instructions on how to pray – so we can be successful at it.

All Power Is From Our Sovereign God

> **... the God of Israel is he that giveth strength and power unto his people ...**
>
> Psalm 68:35 KJV

> **... the excellency of the power may be of God, and not of us ...**
>
> 2 Corinthians 4:7 KJV

Since all power is from God then all we can do is go to God and ask Him for what we want. That is why prayer is called petitioning. This is also why we should trust and rely on Him.

Some petitioners might think that we are able to determine the answers to our prayers through the nature and extend of our praying. Nothing is further from the truth. Our prayers do not determine the answer. God does. Our prayers only determine the nature and extent of our petition.

After all, if our prayers were powerful in terms of determining the results then what role would God have? Prayers do not bypass God and go directly to answers. Prayers go to God first. God provides the answers. That is the order of things. If we try to put it any other way then we try to take God out of the picture. Without God, no prayers get answered.

Let us not forget that without God we cannot do or have anything:

> **I am the vine, ye are the branches: He that abideth in me, and I in him, the same bringeth forth much fruit: for without me ye can do nothing.**
>
> John 15:5 KJV

and

> **A man can receive nothing, except it be given him from heaven.**
>
> John 3:27 KJV

God wants us to realize that we have to come to **the throne of grace ... to find help** (Hebrews 4:16).

Someone might be thinking that prayer could be powerful in terms of getting God to do what we want Him to do. Now think about that. Yes, God yielded to Moses' prayer (Deuteronomy 9:16-29) and to Samson's prayer (Judges 16:18-31). And, yes we can petition God for what we want. But, (A) God is not going to give us anything that is not in His will; and (B) none of us has power over God to make Him do anything. God is sovereign. All we can do is ask.

I believe this is the focal point for understanding prayer and understanding the opening statement about where the real power is. *Since God is a loving God – and He is sovereign and He has all the power then we should rely on Him – and if we rely on him – we must get good at asking.*

Ask God

To be successful at praying, we must be successful at asking. We are told in James 4 that:

... ye have not, because ye ask not ...

and that:

Ye ask, and receive not, because ye ask amiss, that ye may consume it upon your lusts.
James 4:2-3 KJV

God wants us to learn to ask effectively.

Ask According to His Will

I've heard it taught before that we should pray God's Word and His promises. That is, when we pray, we apply God's promises to what we are praying for. This assumes that our petition lines up with God's Word and His promises.

We should pray according to God's will because if it is in His will, He will do it. If it is not in His will, then He will not do it.

And this is the confidence that we have in him, that, if we ask any thing according to his will, he heareth us: And if we know that he hear us, whatsoever we ask, we know that we have the petitions that we desired of him.
1 John 5:14-15 KJV

Praying in God's will was also emphasized when Jesus prayed in the Garden of Gethsemane. He prayed:

"Father, if you are willing, take this cup from me; yet not my will, but yours be done."
Luke 22:42 NIV

Jesus prayed for what He wanted and then said – yet not my will, but your will be done..." Jesus understood that even though He was God in the flesh, the **WILL OF GOD** still had to be done.

The best approach to prayer is to get to know God's will by getting to know God and His Word intimately. This can dramatically impact our prayers in two ways: (1) we know what to pray for, and, (2) as we get closer to God, what we want becomes more like what God wants - because we become more like God.

Seriously meditate on the scriptures below:

Delight yourself in the LORD and he will give you the desires of your heart.
Psalm 37:4 NIV

Jesus taught us that:

Verily, verily, I say unto you, Whatsoever ye shall ask the Father in my name, he will give it you.
John 16:23 KJV

The key phrase is "**in my name.**" Remember, God gave Jesus **the name that is above every name** (Philippians 2:9 NIV). Therefore, what we ask for in Jesus' **name** must line-up with God's will.

Ask Boldly and Persistently

When we ask, God wants us to come to Him **fearlessly and confidently and boldly** (Hebrews 4:16 AMP). Jesus gave us the example of the man who kept knocking on the door of his friend until he got what he wanted:

"Suppose one of you has a friend, and he goes to him at midnight and says, 'Friend, lend me three loaves of bread, because a friend of mine on a journey has come to me, and I have nothing to set before him.'

"Then the one inside answers, 'Don't bother me. The door is already locked, and my children are with me in bed. I can't get up and give you anything.'

I tell you, though he will not get up and give him the bread because he is his friend, yet because of the man's boldness he will get up and give him as much as he needs.

Luke 11:5-8 NIV

In the Parable of the Persistent Widow Jesus taught us to be persistent in asking:

Then Jesus told his disciples a parable to show them that they should always pray and not give up. He said: "In a certain town there was a judge who neither feared God nor cared about men. And there was a widow in that town who kept coming to him with the plea, 'Grant me justice against my adversary.'

"For some time he refused. But finally he said to himself, 'Even though I don't fear God or care about men, yet because this widow keeps bothering me, I will see that she gets justice, so that she won't eventually wear me out with her coming!' "

And the Lord said, "Listen to what the unjust judge says. And will not God bring about justice for his chosen ones, who cry out to him day and night?

Luke 18:1-6 NIV

The approach to prayer has to be persistency. As Jesus said:

> **"And so I tell you, keep on asking, and you will
> receive what you ask for. Keep on seeking, and
> you will find. Keep on knocking, and the door
> will be opened to you. For everyone who asks,
> receives. Everyone who seeks, finds. And to
> everyone who knocks, the door will be opened."**
>
> Luke 11:9-10 NLT

Asking **boldly** and persistently is very important for successful prayer. This point is also underscored in our main scripture, James 5:16. Let us look at it again:

> **The effectual fervent prayer of a righteous man
> availeth much.**
>
> James 5:16 KJV

Earlier we saw that the word **availeth** has to do with the extent to which our prayer pushes or applies force. Now let us examine the words **effectual** and **fervent** which deal with how we pray. Those two words come from the original Greek word **energeō** (#G1754 in the *Strong's Concordance*) which means "to be active, efficient, at work, be mighty." God wants us to engage in **effectual fervent prayer** to Him, prayer that is active, at work and mighty. This means serious prayer, not casual prayer – but mighty prayer.

Some of the synonyms listed for the word **fervent** from *The Roget's New Millennium Thesaurus* at Dictionary.com are ardent, burning, devout, eager, earnest, fiery, glowing, gotta have, gung ho, heartfelt, intense, passionate, serious, sincere, vehement, wholehearted and zealous. Does this describe your prayers?

Gods wants us to pray (or ask) in this manner. If we do, then our prayers will **availeth** or push for what we ask for.

Ask in Faith

God told us to **come boldly unto the throne of grace** (Hebrews 4:16). Part of being bold is to believe you will receive what you pray for. This faith can make you very bold in your prayers (respectfully of course).

Jesus taught:

> **... What things soever ye desire, when ye pray, believe that ye receive them, and ye shall have them.**
>
> Mark 11:24 KJV

Gods wants us to ask **boldly** in faith. In fact, God told us that:

> **If any of you lacks wisdom, he should ask God, who gives generously to all without finding fault, and it will be given to him. But when he asks, he must believe and not doubt, because he who doubts is like a wave of the sea, blown and tossed by the wind. That man should not think he will receive anything from the Lord ...**
>
> James 1:5-7 NIV

If we believe - we receive. But, be careful. Do not take this scripture out of context. Take it in combination with the other scriptures. Your belief has to be in the *will* of our sovereign all-powerful God. Your asking must be in the will of God. When it is, you can come **boldly** and in faith.

Sometimes a lack of faith can be a problem. There was an occasion where Jesus rebuked His disciples for being **faithless** (Matthew 17:17). They were not able to drive a demon out of a boy. Later, Jesus explained how **fasting** with praying could help to bring down Satan's power:

Then came the disciples to Jesus apart, and said, Why could not we cast him out?

And Jesus said unto them, Because of your unbelief: for verily I say unto you, If ye have faith as a grain of mustard seed, ye shall say unto this mountain, Remove hence to yonder place; and it shall remove; and nothing shall be impossible unto you.

Howbeit this kind goeth not out but by prayer and fasting.
Matthew 17:20-21 KJV

Fasting is a denying of the flesh to accomplish a higher call of the Spirit. When properly used, **fasting** can bring us closer to God, especially if used in combination with prayer. In this instance Jesus seems to be telling the disciples that **fasting** would help them improve their **faith**.

Another aspect of getting closer to God is keeping the lines of communication between ourselves and God open so that we stay connected to God.

Keep the Lines of Communication Open

The lines of communication remain open when we have consistency in our prayer life. We are told to:

Pray without ceasing (KJV). Never stop praying (NIV).
1 Thessalonians 5:17

... Praying always with all prayer and supplication in the Spirit ...
Ephesians 6:18 KJV

God told us that if we **seek him** that we will find him (Deuteronomy 4:29; Hebrews 11:6). He is always ready to hear from us. His line is never busy.

Have you ever tried to call someone on the telephone and the line was busy, disconnected or out of range and you could not get your call connected? That will not happen with God if you pray constantly.

One the other hand, have you ever been in a situation where God tried to call you and your line was busy or you were not ready to yield to Him on something? Have you ever been entertaining an evil thought on the other line and could not pick up God's call? It happens. We all fall short at some point.

If we want to keep the lines of communication open with God, then we need to be like Mary (the sister of Martha). Mary had the **one thing** (Luke 10:42). She **sat at the Lord's feet, listening to what he taught** (Luke 10:39 NIV). As a result, Mary had God's attention because she was faithful and she was connected.

When Mary's brother Lazarus died, Mary was patient. She **sat still** (she got alone in prayer) and waited for the call from the Lord (John 11:20, 28-32). When Jesus sent for her, she worshipped **at His feet** and consequently, Jesus was **deeply moved** (John 11:33 NIV).

Mary kept the lines of communication open.

Stayed Connected

Staying connected can help us when we pray. This is why we are told to **never stop praying** (1 Thessalonians 5:17 NIV).

A good example is an electrical cord for a household appliance. If the cord is lying on the floor and is not plugged in - then it will have no power going *through* it. To get the power going, first you have to make the connection by plugging the cord in. Only then can the power begin to surge *through* the cord to the appliance.

We plug in to God through prayer, praise and worship and the knowledge and application of His Word (the Bible).

If you want your prayers answered it not a good idea to wait until you have an urgent prayer request to try to get to know God. But if you spend time in His presence the connection is live and active through a sweet intimacy that can only be maintained through on-going time spent with Him.

As we said earlier:

Delight yourself in the LORD and he will give you the desires of your heart.
Psalm 37:4 NIV

God Hears the Prayers of the Righteous

Another aspect to staying connected to God is like talking on a cell phone. When you have a lot of static sometimes it is difficult to hear what the other person is saying. Or, if you are in a poor reception area and you have only 1 or 2 bars on your cell phone your reception could be impaired. Ideally, you should stay in a good reception area.

In prayer, you want to avoid the hindrances to prayer, those things that can block your prayers from going up and being heard by God. It is best when talking to God that you have five bars so that He will be able to hear your petitions and you will be able to hear what and when He answers you.

In the book, *How to Pray*, by R. A. Torrey, seven hindrances to prayer are explained. We will just list them and some related scriptures here:

1. **Asking amiss**

   Ye ask, and receive not, because ye ask amiss, that ye may consume it upon your lusts.

   James 4:3 KJV

2. **Sin**

   But your iniquities have separated between you and your God, and your sins have hid his face from you, that he will not hear.

   Isaiah 59:2 KJV

   Now we know that God heareth not sinners: but if any man be a worshipper of God, and doeth his will, him he heareth.

   John 9:31 KJV

3. **Idolatry**

   Son of man, these men have set up their idols in their heart, and put the -stumblingblock of their iniquity before their face: should I be enquired of at all by them?

   Ezekiel 14:3 KJV

4. **Stinginess - Not giving to the poor**

   Whoso stoppeth his ears at the cry of the poor, he also shall cry himself, but shall not be heard.

   Proverbs 21:13 KJV

5. **Unforgiving spirit**

   And when ye stand praying, forgive, if ye have ought against any: that your Father also which is in heaven may forgive you your trespasses.

   Mark 11:25 KJV

6. **Wrong relationship between husband and wife**

Likewise, ye husbands, dwell with them according to knowledge, giving honour unto the wife, as unto the weaker vessel, and as being heirs together of the grace of life; that your prayers be not hindered.

1 Peter 3:7 KJV

7. **Unbelief**

If any of you lack wisdom, let him ask of God, that giveth to all men liberally, and upbraideth not; and it shall be given him. But let him ask in faith, nothing wavering. For he that wavereth is like a wave of the sea driven with the wind and tossed. For let not that man think that he shall receive any thing of the Lord.

James 1:5-7 KJV

If you want your prayers to be effective, make sure these hindrances to prayer are not present in your life.

God Taught Us How to Pray

God did not leave us alone to figure out how to pray on our own. He has given us many instructions as well as examples of successful prayer warriors to follow.

Below is a list of instructions from the Bible on how to pray. These scriptures merit a serious study on our part to help us understand how to be effective at praying.

a) What to Pray: The Lord Prayer

I do not believe that the Lord's Prayer was (solely) meant to be recited over and over. I believe Jesus taught us a guide that will help facilitate effective prayer.

> **After this manner therefore pray ye:**
> **Our Father which art in heaven,**
> **Hallowed be thy name.**
> **Thy kingdom come,**
> **Thy will be done in earth,**
> **as it is in heaven.**
> **Give us this day our daily bread.**
> **And forgive us our debts,**
> **as we forgive our debtors.**
> **And lead us not into temptation,**
> **but deliver us from evil:**
> **For thine is the kingdom,**
> **and the power,**
> **and the glory,**
> **for ever. Amen.**
>
> Matthew 6:9-12 KJV

Your challenge is to dissect The Lord's Prayer to see what God is telling you about prayer.

In my view, the Lord's Prayer can be divided into at least seven sections with specific functions of prayer. As a guide, The Lord's Prayer includes at least the following:

(1) Opening, Address to the Father
(2) Praise His Name
(3) Submit to God's Will
(4) Request provision (statement of faith and reliance on God) and intercede for others
(5) Request for forgiveness from God and forgive others

    (6)   Request strength and protection to stay away from evil

    (7)   Thanksgiving

b) When to Pray: Early and Late

O God, thou art my God; early will I seek thee: my soul thirsteth for thee, my flesh longeth for thee in a dry and thirsty land, where no water is; To see thy power and thy glory, so as I have seen thee in the sanctuary.

Psalm 63:1-2 KJV

Very early in the morning, while it was still dark, Jesus got up, left the house and went off to a solitary place, where he prayed.

Mark 1:35 NIV

And when he had sent the multitudes away, he went up into a mountain apart to pray: and when the evening was come, he was there alone.

Matthew 14:23 KJV

c) Where to Pray: In Private (except corporate prayer)

But Jesus often withdrew to lonely places and prayed.

Luke 5:16 NIV

"When you pray, don't be like the hypocrites who love to pray publicly on street corners and in the synagogues where everyone can see them. I tell you the truth, that is all the reward they will ever get. But when you pray, go away by yourself, shut the door behind you, and pray to your Father in private. Then your Father, who sees everything, will reward you."

Matthew 6:5-6 NLT

d) How to Pray: From Your Heart, Come Boldly with Confidence and Faith in Jesus' Name

And when you pray, do not keep on babbling like pagans, for they think they will be heard because of their many words. Do not be like them, for your Father knows what you need before you ask him.

Matthew 6:6-7 NIV

Let us then fearlessly and confidently and boldly draw near to the throne of grace (the throne of God's unmerited favor to us sinners), that we may receive mercy [for our failures] and find grace to help in good time for every need [appropriate help and well-timed help, coming just when we need it].

Hebrews 4:16 AMP

Therefore I say unto you, What things soever ye desire, when ye pray, believe that ye receive them, and ye shall have them.

Mark 11:24 KJV

Verily, verily, I say unto you, Whatsoever ye shall ask the Father in my name, he will give it you.

John 16:23 KJV

e) How Long to Pray: One Hour, Persistently, Without Ceasing

And he cometh unto the disciples, and findeth them asleep, and saith unto Peter, What, could ye not watch with me one hour? Watch and pray, that ye enter not into temptation: the spirit indeed is willing, but the flesh is weak.

Matthew 26:40-41 KJV

For a friend of mine who is on a journey has just come, and I have nothing to put before him; And he from within will answer, Do not disturb me; the door is now closed, and my children are with me in bed; I cannot get up and supply you [with anything]? I tell you, although he will not get up and supply him anything because he is his friend, yet because of his shameless persistence and insistence he will get up and give him as much as he needs. So I say to you, Ask and keep on asking and it shall be given you; seek and keep on seeking and you shall find; knock and keep on knocking and the door shall be opened to you.

Luke 11:6-8 AMP

[The Parable of the Persistent Widow] Then Jesus told his disciples a parable to show them that they should always pray and not give up.

Luke 18:1 NIV

And it came to pass in those days, that he went out into a mountain to pray, and continued all night in prayer to God.

Luke 6:12 KJV

Pray without ceasing (KJV). Never stop praying (NIV).

1 Thessalonians 5:17

f) How Often to Pray: Every Day, Always, Three Times a Day

Give us this day our daily bread.

Matthew 6:11 KJV

Now when Daniel knew that the writing was signed, he went into his house; and his windows being open in his chamber toward Jerusalem, he kneeled upon his knees three times a day, and prayed, and gave thanks before his God, as he did aforetime.

Daniel 6:10 KJV

Praying always with all prayer and supplication in the Spirit ...

Ephesians 6:18 KJV

g) Who Should We Pray For: Ourselves, Others, Leaders, All the Saints

I exhort therefore, that, first of all, supplications, prayers, intercessions, and giving of thanks, be made for all men; For kings, and for all that are in authority; that we may lead a quiet and peaceable life in all godliness and honesty.

1 Timothy 2:1-2 KJV

Confess your faults one to another, and pray one for another, that ye may be healed.
James 5:16 KJV

... and watching thereunto with all perseverance and supplication for all saints
Ephesians 6:18 KJV

Let us then fearlessly and confidently and boldly draw near to the throne of grace (the throne of God's unmerited favor to us sinners), that we may receive mercy [for our failures] and find grace to help in good time for every need [appropriate help and well-timed help, coming just when we need it].
Hebrews 4:16 AMP

The Story of Daniel Gives Us an Example of a Successful Prayer Life

Daniel was a faithful man. We know that he prayed three times a day (Daniel 6:10) and did not defile himself with the king's meat and wine (Daniel 1:8-20). The Bible tells us that Daniel's prayer involved getting **down on his knees ... giving thanks to His God ... and asking for God's help** (Daniel 6:10-11 NIV). He also fasted (Daniel 9:3; 10:3). He praised God, confessed sins and interceded (Daniel 9).

I am sure that his prayer life contributed to his success both spiritually and in the world. Prayer enabled him to maintain his holiness while being in a high position of government in Babylon.

There are four points to note about Daniel 's walk with God that are directly attributable to his prayer life:

First, The Bible tells us that there was an **excellent spirit** in Daniel (Daniel 5:12; 6:3) which of course came from the Lord.

How did Daniel get this **excellent spirit**? He stayed connected to the Lord through prayer.

Second, the Lord protected Daniel. When Daniel was thrown into the Lion's den he came out unharmed – because he was connected to God through prayer.

> **My God sent his angel, and he shut the mouths of the lions. They have not hurt me, because I was found innocent in his sight ..."**
>
> Daniel 6:21-22 NIV

Third, even though spiritual opposition caused Daniel to experience delay in getting certain of his prayers answered, those answers eventually came (Daniel 10:10-14). During the delay, Daniel continued to pray as was his usual practice (Daniel 6:10; 9; 10).

Four, God gave Daniel great visions and revelations (Daniel 7-10). Daniel was prepared to hear from the Lord because the lines of communication were open between him and God, the result of his prayer life and his holiness.

If we follow Daniel's example, then like Daniel, each of us can have an **excellent spirit** in us, be protected by the Lord, get answers to our prayers even when/if there is spiritual opposition, and experience great revelations from the Lord.

God tells us that anyone who obeys His Word is on solid ground:

> **Anyone who comes and listens to me and obeys me is like someone who dug down deep and built a house on solid rock. When the flood came and the river rushed against the house, it was built so well that it didn't even shake.**
>
> Luke 6:47-48 CEV

"...your heavenly Father is even more ready to give the Holy Spirit to anyone who asks..."
Luke 11:13 CEV

Listen to what God says in His Word about prayer - then obey. You too will be on solid ground and be victorious Like Daniel.

Epilogue

When you look at the great men of God you will see that they were all men of prayer. Noah was the **only blameless person living on earth at the time, and he walked in close fellowship with God** (Genesis 6:9 NLT). Abraham, **the friend of God** (James 2:23), constantly prayed and sacrificed to Our Lord. David**, a man after his** [God's] **own heart** (1 Samuel 13:13-14 KJV), wrote many of the Psalms and **danced** [in worship] **before the LORD with all his might** (2 Samuel 6:13-21). Moses' spent countless hours before the Lord. In fact, his **face was shining brightly because the LORD had been speaking to him** (Exodus 34:29-35 CEV).

Nonetheless, all of these great men of God were human. One of the things you should notice about this select group of Godly warriors is that, like all of us, they all had shortcomings. When they acted in their own strength (or power) they made huge errors! Noah got drunk and passed out (Genesis 9:20-24). David committed adultery and murder (2 Samuel 11). Moses murdered a man and had bouts of anger, consequently he missed the Promised Land (Exodus 2:11-16; Number 20:2-13). Abraham created a nation of rebels through his unbelief and his act with Hagar (Genesis 16:1-4; 17:19-20; Galatians 4:23).

What's the point? When they stayed connected to God, when they were obedient to God, when their actions were determined through their prayer life – when they operated in God's *will* and His **power** - they did great things for God. But when they operated in their own strength and understanding (see Proverbs 3:5-6) they messed up big time.

If you want real power in your life – stay connected to God through **fervent prayer** and stay in His will. He's got the **power** and He alone will use it.

Just ASK GOD.

Lessons
on Prayers
From the Bible

The House of Prayer

Luke 19:46 KJV

It is written, My house is the house of prayer ...

Ask, Seek and Knock

Matthew 7:8-12 NIV

For everyone who asks receives; he who seeks finds; and to him who knocks, the door will be opened.

"Which of you, if his son asks for bread, will give him a stone? Or if he asks for a fish, will give him a snake? If you, then, though you are evil, know how to give good gifts to your children, how much more will your Father in heaven give good gifts to those who ask him! So in everything, do to others what you would have them do to you, for this sums up the Law and the Prophets.

Luke 11:9-13 AMP

So I say to you, Ask and keep on asking and it shall be given you; seek and keep on seeking and you shall find; knock and keep on knocking and the door shall be opened to you.

For everyone who asks and keeps on asking receives; and he who seeks and keeps on seeking finds; and to him who knocks and keeps on knocking, the door shall be opened.

What father among you, if his son asks for a loaf of bread, will give him a stone; or if he asks for a fish, will instead of a fish give him a serpent?

Or if he asks for an egg, will give him a scorpion?

If you then, evil as you are, know how to give good gifts [gifts that are to their advantage] to your children, how much more will your heavenly Father give the Holy Spirit to those who ask and continue to ask Him!

Believe When You Pray

Mark 11:20-25 NIV

In the morning, as they went along, they saw the fig tree withered from the roots. Peter remembered and said to Jesus, "Rabbi, look! The fig tree you cursed has withered!"

"Have faith in God," Jesus answered. "I tell you the truth, if anyone says to this mountain, 'Go, throw yourself into the sea,' and does not doubt in his heart but believes that what he says will happen, it will be done for him. Therefore I tell you, whatever you ask for in prayer, believe that you have received it, and it will be yours. And when you stand praying, if you hold anything against anyone, forgive him, so that your Father in heaven may forgive you your sins."

Early Will I Seek You

Mark 1:35 NIV

Very early in the morning, while it was still dark, Jesus got up, left the house and went off to a solitary place, where he prayed.

Psalm 63:1 KJV

O God, thou art my God; early will I seek thee:
> my soul thirsteth for thee,
> my flesh longeth for thee in a dry and thirsty land,
> where no water is.

Psalm 119:147-148 NIV

I rise before dawn and cry for help;
> I have put my hope in your word.
My eyes stay open through the watches of the night,
> that I may meditate on your promises.

Psalm 5:3 AMP

In the morning You hear my voice, O Lord;

in the morning I prepare [a prayer, a sacrifice] for You

and watch and wait [for You to speak to my heart].

Jesus Taught Us the Lord's Prayer

Matthew 6:5-18 NLT

"When you pray, don't be like the hypocrites who love to pray publicly on street corners and in the synagogues where everyone can see them. I tell you the truth, that is all the reward they will ever get. But when you pray, go away by yourself, shut the door behind you, and pray to your Father in private. Then your Father, who sees everything, will reward you.

"When you pray, don't babble on and on as people of other religions do. They think their prayers are answered merely by repeating their words again and again. Don't be like them, for your Father knows exactly what you need even before you ask him! Pray like this:

Our Father in heaven,
may your name be kept holy.
May your Kingdom come soon.
May your will be done on earth,
as it is in heaven.
Give us today the food we need,
and forgive us our sins,
as we have forgiven those who sin against us.
And don't let us yield to temptation,
but rescue us from the evil one.

"If you forgive those who sin against you, your heavenly Father will forgive you. But if you refuse to forgive others, your Father will not forgive your sins.

"And when you fast, don't make it obvious, as the hypocrites do, for they try to look miserable and disheveled so people will admire them for their fasting. I tell you the truth, that is the only reward they will ever get. But when you fast, comb your hair and wash your face. Then no one will notice that you are fasting, except your Father, who knows what you do in private. And your Father, who sees everything, will reward you."

Come Boldly to the Throne of Grace

Hebrews 4:13-16 KJV

Neither is there any creature that is not manifest in his sight: but all things are naked and opened unto the eyes of him with whom we have to do.

Seeing then that we have a great high priest, that is passed into the heavens, Jesus the Son of God, let us hold fast our profession.

For we have not an high priest which cannot be touched with the feeling of our infirmities; but was in all points tempted like as we are, yet without sin.

Let us therefore come boldly unto the throne of grace, that we may obtain mercy, and find grace to help in time of need.

Seven Hindrances to Prayer

1. Unforgiving spirit - Mark: 11:25-26 KJV

And when ye stand praying, forgive, if ye have ought against any: that your Father also which is in heaven may forgive you your trespasses. But if ye do not forgive, neither will your Father which is in heaven forgive your trespasses.

2. Wrong Relationship Between Husband and Wife - 1 Peter 3:7 AMP

In the same way you married men should live considerately with [your wives], with an intelligent recognition [of the marriage relation], honoring the woman as [physically] the weaker, but [realizing that you] are joint heirs of the grace (God's unmerited favor) of life, in order that your prayers may not be hindered and cut off. [Otherwise you cannot pray effectively.]

3.   Sin

Psalm 66:18 NIV

If I had cherished sin in my heart, the Lord would not have listened.

Isaiah 59:1-2 KJV

Behold, the LORD's hand is not shortened, that it cannot save; neither his ear heavy, that it cannot hear:

But your iniquities have separated between you and your God, and your sins have hid his face from you, that he will not hear.

Proverbs 15:29 NIV

The LORD is far from the wicked but he hears the prayer of the righteous.

4.   Not Giving to the Poor - Proverbs 21:13 NLT

Those who shut their ears to the cries of the poor
will be ignored in their own time of need.

5.   Asking Amiss (with Wrong Motives) - James 4:3 NIV

When you ask, you do not receive, because you ask with wrong motives, that you may spend what you get on your pleasures.

6.   Unbelief - James 1:5-7 KJV

If any of you lack wisdom, let him ask of God, that giveth to all men liberally, and upbraideth not; and it shall be given him.

But let him ask in faith, nothing wavering. For he that wavereth is like a wave of the sea driven with the wind and tossed.

For let not that man think that he shall receive any thing of the Lord.

7. Idolatry - Ezekiel 14:3 NIV

Son of man, these men have set up idols in their hearts and put wicked stumbling blocks before their faces. Should I let them inquire of me at all?

Thanksgiving and Prayer

2 Thessalonians 1:3-12 NIV

We ought always to thank God for you, brothers, and rightly so, because your faith is growing more and more, and the love every one of you has for each other is increasing. Therefore, among God's churches we boast about your perseverance and faith in all the persecutions and trials you are enduring.

All this is evidence that God's judgment is right, and as a result you will be counted worthy of the kingdom of God, for which you are suffering. God is just: He will pay back trouble to those who trouble you and give relief to you who are troubled, and to us as well. This will happen when the Lord Jesus is revealed from heaven in blazing fire with his powerful angels. He will punish those who do not know God and do not obey the gospel of our Lord Jesus. They will be punished with everlasting destruction and shut out from the presence of the Lord and from the majesty of his power on the day he comes to be glorified in his holy people and to be marveled at among all those who have believed. This includes you, because you believed our testimony to you.

With this in mind, we constantly pray for you, that our God may count you worthy of his calling, and that by his power he may fulfill every good purpose of yours and every act prompted by your faith. We pray this so that the name of our Lord Jesus may be glorified in you, and you in him, according to the grace of our God and the Lord Jesus Christ.

Pray for Others

Job 42:10 AMP

And the Lord turned the captivity of Job and restored his fortunes, when he prayed for his friends; also the Lord gave Job twice as much as he had before.

1 Timothy 2:1-2 KJV

I exhort therefore, that, first of all, supplications, prayers, intercessions, and giving of thanks, be made for all men;

For kings, and for all that are in authority; that we may lead a quiet and peaceable life in all godliness and honesty.

Ephesians 6:18-19 NIV

And pray in the Spirit on all occasions with all kinds of prayers and requests. With this in mind, be alert and always keep on praying for all the saints.

Pray also for me, that whenever I open my mouth, words may be given me so that I will fearlessly make known the mystery of the gospel,

James 5:15 AMP

Confess to one another therefore your faults (your slips, your false steps, your offenses, your sins) and pray [also] for one another, that you may be healed and restored [to a spiritual tone of mind and heart]. The earnest (heartfelt, continued) prayer of a righteous man makes tremendous power available [dynamic in its working].

Prayer of Faith

James 5:13-16 KJV

Is any among you afflicted? let him pray. Is any merry? let him sing psalms.

Is any sick among you? let him call for the elders of the church; and let them pray over him, anointing him with oil in the name of the Lord:

And the prayer of faith shall save the sick, and the Lord shall raise him up; and if he have committed sins, they shall be forgiven him.

Confess your faults one to another, and pray one for another, that ye may be healed. The effectual fervent prayer of a righteous man availeth much.

James 5:13-16 KJV

Is any one of you in trouble? He should pray. Is anyone happy? Let him sing songs of praise.

Is any one of you sick? He should call the elders of the church to pray over him and anoint him with oil in the name of the Lord.

And the prayer offered in faith will make the sick person well; the Lord will raise him up. If he has sinned, he will be forgiven.

Therefore confess your sins to each other and pray for each other so that you may be healed. The prayer of a righteous man is powerful and effective.

James 5:13-16 AMP

Is anyone among you afflicted (ill-treated, suffering evil)? He should pray. Is anyone glad at heart? He should sing praise [to God].

Is anyone among you sick? He should call in the church elders (the spiritual guides). And they should pray over him, anointing him with oil in the Lord's name.

And the prayer [that is] of faith will save him who is sick, and the Lord will restore him; and if he has committed sins, he will be forgiven.

Confess to one another therefore your faults (your slips, your false steps, your offenses, your sins) and pray [also] for one another, that you may be healed and restored [to a spiritual tone of mind and heart]. The earnest (heartfelt, continued) prayer of a righteous man makes tremendous power available [dynamic in its working].

Pray Continuously

Ephesians 6:18-20 KJV

Praying always with all prayer and supplication in the Spirit, and watching thereunto with all perseverance and supplication for all saints;

And for me, that utterance may be given unto me, that I may open my mouth boldly, to make known the mystery of the gospel,

For which I am an ambassador in bonds: that therein I may speak boldly, as I ought to speak.

Ephesians 6:18-20 NIV

And pray in the Spirit on all occasions with all kinds of prayers and requests. With this in mind, be alert and always keep on praying for all the saints.

Pray also for me, that whenever I open my mouth, words may be given me so that I will fearlessly make known the mystery of the gospel, for which I am an ambassador in chains. Pray that I may declare it fearlessly, as I should.

Ephesians 6:18-20 NLT

Pray in the Spirit at all times and on every occasion. Stay alert and be persistent in your prayers for all believers everywhere.

And pray for me, too. Ask God to give me the right words so I can boldly explain God's mysterious plan that the Good News is for Jews and Gentiles alike. I am in chains now, still preaching this message as God's ambassador. So pray that I will keep on speaking boldly for him, as I should.

Prayers in the Bible

1. Abijah Prayed for Victory Over Jeroboam

2 Chronicles 13:1-18 KJV

Abijah set the battle in array with an army of valiant men of war, even four hundred thousand chosen men: Jeroboam ... with eight hundred thousand chosen men, being mighty men of valour.

And Abijah stood up upon mount Zemaraim ... said, Hear me, thou Jeroboam, and all Israel; Ought ye not to know that the LORD God of Israel gave the kingdom over Israel to David for ever ... Yet Jeroboam the son of Nebat, the servant of Solomon the son of David, is risen up, and hath rebelled against his lord ... Have ye not cast out the priests of the LORD, the sons of Aaron, and the Levites, and have made you priests after the manner of the nations of other lands? ... the LORD is our God, and we have not forsaken him; and the priests, which minister unto the LORD, are the sons of Aaron, and the Levites wait upon their business:

And they burn unto the LORD every morning and every evening burnt sacrifices and sweet incense: the shewbread also set they in order upon the pure table; and the candlestick of gold with the lamps thereof, to burn every evening: for we keep the charge of the LORD our God; ... God himself is with us for our captain, and his priests with sounding trumpets to cry alarm against you. O children of Israel, fight ye not against the LORD God of your fathers; for ye shall not prosper.

But Jeroboam caused an ambushment to come about behind them: so they were before Judah, and the ambushment was behind them.

... when Judah looked back, behold, the battle was before and behind: and they cried unto the LORD, and the priests sounded with the trumpets. Then the men of Judah gave a shout: and as the men of Judah shouted, it came to pass, that God smote Jeroboam and all Israel before Abijah and Judah.

And the children of Israel fled before Judah: and God delivered them into their hand ... great slaughter: so there fell down five hundred thousand chosen men ... the children of Judah prevailed, because they relied upon the LORD God of their fathers.

2. Abraham Prayed for an Heir

Genesis 15: 1-6 KJV

After these things the word of the LORD came unto Abram in a vision, saying, Fear not, Abram: I am thy shield, and thy exceeding great reward.

And Abram said, LORD God, what wilt thou give me, seeing I go childless, and the steward of my house is this Eliezer of Damascus?

And Abram said, Behold, to me thou hast given no seed: and, lo, one born in my house is mine heir.

And, behold, the word of the LORD came unto him, saying, This shall not be thine heir; but he that shall come forth out of thine own bowels shall be thine heir.

And he brought him forth abroad, and said, Look now toward heaven, and tell the stars, if thou be able to number them: and he said unto him, So shall thy seed be.

And he believed in the LORD; and he counted it to him for righteousness.

Romans 4:18-22 AMP

[For Abraham, human reason for] hope being gone, hoped in faith that he should become the father of many nations, as he had been promised, So [numberless] shall your descendants be.

He did not weaken in faith when he considered the [utter] impotence of his own body, which was as good as dead because he was about a hundred years old, or [when he considered] the barrenness of Sarah's [deadened] womb.

No unbelief or distrust made him waver (doubtingly question) concerning the promise of God, but he grew strong and was empowered by faith as he gave praise and glory to God,

Fully satisfied and assured that God was able and mighty to keep His word and to do what He had promised.

That is why his faith was credited to him as righteousness (right standing with God).

3. Abraham Prayed for Sodom & Gomorrah

Genesis 18:20-33 KJV

And the LORD said, Because the cry of Sodom and Gomorrah is great, and because their sin is very grievous;

I will go down now, and see whether they have done altogether according to the cry of it, which is come unto me; and if not, I will know.

And the men turned their faces from thence, and went toward Sodom: but Abraham stood yet before the LORD.

And Abraham drew near, and said, Wilt thou also destroy the righteous with the wicked?

Peradventure there be fifty righteous within the city: wilt thou also destroy and not spare the place for the fifty righteous that are therein?

That be far from thee to do after this manner, to slay the righteous with the wicked: and that the righteous should be as the wicked, that be far from thee: Shall not the Judge of all the earth do right?

And the LORD said, If I find in Sodom fifty righteous within the city, then I will spare all the place for their sakes.

And Abraham answered and said, Behold now, I have taken upon me to speak unto the LORD, which am but dust and ashes:

Peradventure there shall lack five of the fifty righteous: wilt thou destroy all the city for lack of five? And he said, If I find there forty and five, I will not destroy it.

And he spake unto him yet again, and said, Peradventure there shall be forty found there. And he said, I will not do it for forty's sake.

And he said unto him, Oh let not the LORD be angry, and I will speak: Peradventure there shall thirty be found there. And he said, I will not do it, if I find thirty there.

And he said, Behold now, I have taken upon me to speak unto the LORD: Peradventure there shall be twenty found there. And he said, I will not destroy it for twenty's sake.

And he said, Oh let not the LORD be angry, and I will speak yet but this once: Peradventure ten shall be found there. And he said, I will not destroy it for ten's sake.

And the LORD went his way, as soon as he had left communing with Abraham: and Abraham returned unto his place.

4. Abraham Prayed for Abimelech & His Wife

Genesis 17:1-20 KJV

... Abraham journeyed ... south country, and dwelled between Kadesh and Shur, and sojourned in Gerar. And Abraham said of Sarah his wife, She is my sister: and Abimelech king of Gerar sent, and took Sarah.

... God came to Abimelech in a dream by night ... Behold, thou art but a dead man, for the woman which thou hast taken; for she is a man's wife. But Abimelech had not come near her: and he said, LORD, wilt thou slay also a righteous nation? Said he not unto me, She is my sister? ... even she herself said, He is my brother: in the integrity of my heart and innocency of my hands ... God said unto him in a dream, Yea, I know that thou didst this in the integrity of thy heart; for I also withheld thee from sinning against me: therefore suffered I thee not to touch her ... restore the man his wife; for he is a prophet, and he shall pray for thee, and thou shalt live: and if thou restore her not, know thou that thou shalt surely die, thou, and all that are thine.

… Abimelech rose early in the morning, and called all his servants, and told all these things in their ears: and the men were sore afraid.

Then Abimelech called Abraham, and said unto him, What hast thou done unto us? and what have I offended thee, that thou hast brought on me and on my kingdom a great sin? thou hast done deeds unto me that ought not to be done … And Abraham said, Because I thought, Surely the fear of God is not in this place; and they will slay me for my wife's sake.

And yet indeed she is my sister; she is the daughter of my father, but not the daughter of my mother; and she became my wife.

And it came to pass, when God caused me to wander from my father's house, that I said unto her, This is thy kindness which thou shalt shew unto me; at every place whither we shall come, say of me, He is my brother.

… Abimelech took sheep, oxen, menservants, womenservants, gave unto Abraham, and restored him Sarah his wife… said, Behold, my land is before thee: dwell where it pleaseth thee … unto Sarah he said, Behold, I have given thy brother a thousand pieces of silver: behold, he is to thee a covering of the eyes, unto all that are with thee, and with all other: thus she was reproved.

So Abraham prayed unto God: and God healed Abimelech, and his wife, and his maidservants; and they bare children. For the LORD had fast closed up all the wombs of the house of Abimelech, because of Sarah Abraham's wife.

5.   Abraham prayed for Ishmael

Genesis 17:18-21 KJV

And Abraham said unto God, O that Ishmael might live before thee!

And God said, Sarah thy wife shall bear thee a son indeed; and thou shalt call his name Isaac: and I will establish my covenant with him for an everlasting covenant, and with his seed after him.

And as for Ishmael, I have heard thee: Behold, I have blessed him, and will make him fruitful, and will multiply him exceedingly; twelve princes shall he beget, and I will make him a great nation.

But my covenant will I establish with Isaac, which Sarah shall bear unto thee at this set time in the next year.

6. Ananias Lays Hands on Saul

Acts 9:10-17 NIV

In Damascus there was a disciple named Ananias. The Lord called to him in a vision, "Ananias!"

"Yes, Lord," he answered.

The Lord told him, "Go to the house of Judas on Straight Street and ask for a man from Tarsus named Saul, for he is praying. 12In a vision he has seen a man named Ananias come and place his hands on him to restore his sight."

"Lord," Ananias answered, "I have heard many reports about this man and all the harm he has done to your saints in Jerusalem. 14And he has come here with authority from the chief priests to arrest all who call on your name."

But the Lord said to Ananias, "Go! This man is my chosen instrument to carry my name before the Gentiles and their kings and before the people of Israel. 16I will show him how much he must suffer for my name."

Then Ananias went to the house and entered it. Placing his hands on Saul, he said, "Brother Saul, the Lord—Jesus, who appeared to you on the road as you were coming here—has sent me so that you may see again and be filled with the Holy Spirit." Immediately, something like scales fell from Saul's eyes, and he could see again. He got up and was baptized, and after taking some food, he regained his strength.

7.   Apostles Pray for Guidance

Act 1:12-16 CEV

The Mount of Olives was about half a mile from Jerusalem. The apostles who had gone there were Peter, John, James, Andrew, Philip, Thomas, Bartholomew, Matthew, James the son of Alphaeus, Simon, known as the Eager One, and Judas the son of James. After the apostles returned to the city, they went upstairs to the room where they had been staying.

The apostles often met together and prayed with a single purpose in mind. The women and Mary the mother of Jesus would meet with them, and so would his brothers. One day there were about one hundred twenty of the Lord's followers meeting together, and Peter stood up to speak to them ... My friends, long ago by the power of the Holy Spirit, David said something about Judas, and what he said has now happened.

Judas was one of us and had worked with us, but he brought the mob to arrest Jesus. Then Judas bought some land with the money he was given for doing that evil thing. He fell headfirst into the field. His body burst open, and all his insides came out. When the people of Jerusalem found out about this, they called the place Akeldama, which in the local language means "Field of Blood."

In the book of Psalms it says,

"Leave his house empty, and don't let anyone live there."

It also says, "Let someone else have his job."

So we need someone else to help us tell others that Jesus has been raised from death. He must also be one of the men who was with us from the very beginning. He must have been with us from the time the Lord Jesus was baptized by John until the day he was taken to heaven.

Two men were suggested: One of them was Joseph Barsabbas, known as Justus, and the other was Matthias. Then they all prayed, "Lord, you know what everyone is like! Show us the one you have chosen to be an apostle and to serve in place of

Judas, who got what he deserved." They drew names, and Matthias was chosen to join the group of the eleven apostles.

8. Apostles Believer's Prayer

Acts 4:1-31 NIV

The priests and the captain of the temple guard and the Sadducees came up to Peter and John while they were speaking to the people. They were greatly disturbed because the apostles were teaching the people and proclaiming in Jesus the resurrection of the dead. They seized Peter and John, and because it was evening, they put them in jail until the next day. But many who heard the message believed, and the number of men grew to about five thousand ...

Then Peter, filled with the Holy Spirit, said to them: "Rulers and elders of the people! If we are being called to account today for an act of kindness shown to a cripple and are asked how he was healed, then know this, you and all the people of Israel: It is by the name of Jesus Christ of Nazareth ...

When they saw the courage of Peter and John and realized that they were unschooled, ordinary men, they were astonished and they took note that these men had been with Jesus. But since they could see the man who had been healed standing there with them, there was nothing they could say ...

On their release, Peter and John went back to their own people and reported all that the chief priests and elders had said to them. When they heard this, they raised their voices together in prayer to God. "Sovereign Lord," they said, "you made the heaven and the earth and the sea, and everything in them. You spoke by the Holy Spirit through the mouth of your servant, our father David:

"'Why do the nations rage and the peoples plot in vain? The kings of the earth take their stand and the rulers gather together against the Lord and against his Anointed One. Indeed Herod and Pontius Pilate met together with the Gentiles and the people of

Israel in this city to conspire against your holy servant Jesus, whom you anointed. They did what your power and will had decided beforehand should happen. Now, Lord, consider their threats and enable your servants to speak your word with great boldness. Stretch out your hand to heal and perform miraculous signs and wonders through the name of your holy servant Jesus."

After they prayed, the place where they were meeting was shaken. And they were all filled with the Holy Spirit and spoke the word of God boldly.

9.   Children of Israel Cried Unto the Lord in Egypt

Exodus 2:23-25 KJV

And it came to pass in process of time, that the king of Egypt died: and the children of Israel sighed by reason of the bondage, and they cried, and their cry came up unto God by reason of the bondage.

And God heard their groaning, and God remembered his covenant with Abraham, with Isaac, and with Jacob. And God looked upon the children of Israel, and God had respect unto them.

10. Children of Israel Cried Unto the Lord at the Red Sea

Exodus 14:10

And when Pharaoh drew nigh, the children of Israel lifted up their eyes, and, behold, the Egyptians marched after them; and they were sore afraid: and the children of Israel cried out unto the LORD.

11. Children of Israel Cried Unto the Lord in Mesopotamia

Judges 3:8-10 KJV

… the anger of the LORD was hot against Israel, and he sold them into the hand of Chushanrishathaim king of Mesopotamia … Israel served Chushanrishathaim eight years.

And when the children of Israel cried unto the LORD, the LORD raised up a deliverer … Othniel the son of Kenaz, Caleb's younger brother. And the Spirit of the LORD came upon him, and he judged Israel, and went out to war: and the LORD delivered … king of Mesopotamia into his hand …

12. Children of Israel Cried Unto the Lord under the Ling of Moab

Judges 3:14-21 KJV

… children of Israel served Eglon the king of Moab eighteen years.

… when the children of Israel cried unto the LORD, the LORD raised them up a deliverer, Ehud the son of Gera, a Benjamite, a man lefthanded: and by him the children of Israel sent a present unto Eglon the king of Moab. But Ehud made him a dagger which had two edges, of a cubit length; and he did gird it under his raiment upon his right thigh. … he brought the present unto Eglon king of Moab … a very fat man … Ehud put forth his left hand … took the dagger … and thrust it into his belly:

13. Church Prayed & Fasted for Paul & Barnabas

Acts 13:1-3 AMP

Now in the church (assembly) at Antioch there were prophets (inspired interpreters of the will and purposes of God) and teachers: Barnabas, Symeon who was called Niger [Black], Lucius of Cyrene, Manaen a member of the court of Herod the tetrarch, and Saul.

While they were worshiping the Lord and fasting, the Holy Spirit said, Separate now for Me Barnabas and Saul for the work to which I have called them.

Then after fasting and praying, they put their hands on them and sent them away.

Acts 13:1-3 NLT

Among the prophets and teachers of the church at Antioch of Syria were Barnabas, Simeon (called "the black man"), Lucius (from Cyrene), Manaen (the childhood companion of King Herod Antipas), and Saul.

One day as these men were worshiping the Lord and fasting, the Holy Spirit said, "Dedicate Barnabas and Saul for the special work to which I have called them."

So after more fasting and prayer, the men laid their hands on them and sent them on their way.

14. Church Prayed for Peter

Act 12:1-16 KJV

Now about that time Herod the king stretched forth his hands to vex certain of the church. And he killed James the brother of John with the sword.

And because he saw it pleased the Jews, he proceeded further to take Peter also. (Then were the days of unleavened bread.)

And when he had apprehended him, he put him in prison, and delivered him to four quaternions of soldiers to keep him; intending after Easter to bring him forth to the people.

Peter therefore was kept in prison: but prayer was made without ceasing of the church unto God for him. And when Herod would have brought him forth, the same night Peter was sleeping between two soldiers, bound with two chains: and the keepers before the door kept the prison.

And, behold, the angel of the Lord came upon him, and a light shined in the prison: and he smote Peter on the side, and raised him up, saying, Arise up quickly. And his chains fell off from his hands.

And the angel said unto him, Gird thyself, and bind on thy sandals. And so he did. And he saith unto him, Cast thy garment about thee, and follow me.

And he went out, and followed him; and wist not that it was true which was done by the angel; but thought he saw a vision.

When they were past the first and the second ward, they came unto the iron gate that leadeth unto the city; which opened to them of his own accord: and they went out, and passed on through one street; and forthwith the angel departed from him.

And when Peter was come to himself, he said, Now I know of a surety, that the LORD hath sent his angel, and hath delivered me out of the hand of Herod, and from all the expectation of the people of the Jews.

And when he had considered the thing, he came to the house of Mary the mother of John, whose surname was Mark; where many were gathered together praying. And as Peter knocked at the door of the gate, a damsel came to hearken, named Rhoda. And when she knew Peter's voice, she opened not the gate for gladness, but ran in, and told how Peter stood before the gate.

And they said unto her, Thou art mad. But she constantly affirmed that it was even so. Then said they, It is his angel.

But Peter continued knocking: and when they had opened the door, and saw him, they were astonished.

15. Cornelius & Peter Pray for Enlightenment

Act 10:1-5, 9, 15, 23-25, 27-28, 30-33, 34-36, 44 NIV

At Caesarea there was a man named Cornelius, a centurion in what was known as the Italian Regiment. He and all his family were devout and God-fearing; he gave generously to those in need and prayed to God regularly. One day at about three in the afternoon he had a vision. He distinctly saw an angel of God, who came to him and said, "Cornelius!"

Cornelius stared at him in fear. "What is it, Lord?" he asked.

The angel answered, "Your prayers and gifts to the poor have come up as a memorial offering before God. Now send men to Joppa to bring back a man named Simon who is called Peter ...

About noon the following day as they were on their journey and approaching the city, Peter went up on the roof to pray ...

The voice spoke to him a second time, "Do not call anything impure that God has made clean." ...

The next day Peter started out with them, and some of the brothers from Joppa went along. The following day he arrived in Caesarea. Cornelius was expecting them and had called together his relatives and close friends. As Peter entered the house, Cornelius met him ...

Peter went inside and found a large gathering of people. He said to them: "You are well aware that it is against our law for a Jew to associate with a Gentile or visit him. But God has shown me that I should not call any man impure or unclean ...

Cornelius answered: "Four days ago I was in my house praying at this hour, at three in the afternoon. Suddenly a man in shining clothes stood before me and said, 'Cornelius, God has heard your prayer and remembered your gifts to the poor. Send to Joppa for Simon who is called Peter ... Now we are all here in the presence of God to listen to everything the Lord has commanded you to tell us ...

Then Peter began to speak: "I now realize how true it is that God does not show favoritism but accepts men from every nation who fear him and do what is right. You know the message God sent to the people of Israel, telling the good news of peace through Jesus Christ, who is Lord of all ... While Peter was still speaking these words, the Holy Spirit came on all who heard the message.

16. Daniel Prayed Three Times a Day

Daniel 6:10:26 KJV

Now when Daniel knew that the writing was signed, he went into his house; and his windows being open in his chamber toward Jerusalem, he kneeled upon his knees three times a day, and prayed, and gave thanks before his God, as he did aforetime.

Then these men assembled, and found Daniel praying and making supplication before his God. Then they came near, and spake before the king ... Hast thou not signed a decree, that every man that shall ask a petition of any God or man within thirty days ... shall be cast into the den of lions? ... Daniel, which is of the children of the captivity of Judah, regardeth not thee, O king, nor the decree that thou hast signed, but maketh his petition three times a day.

Then the king ... was sore displeased with himself, and set his heart on Daniel to deliver him: and he laboured till the going down of the sun to deliver him.

Then these men assembled unto the king, and said unto the king, Know, O king, that the law of the Medes and Persians is, That no decree nor statute which the king establisheth may be changed. Then the king commanded, and they brought Daniel, and cast him into the den of lions. Now the king spake and said unto Daniel, Thy God whom thou servest continually, he will deliver thee … a stone was brought, and laid upon the mouth of the den; and the king sealed it with his own signet, and with the signet of his lords; that the purpose might not be changed concerning Daniel.

Then the king went to his palace, and passed the night fasting: neither were instruments of musick brought before him: and his sleep went from him. Then the king arose very early in the morning, and went in haste unto the den of lions.

And when he came to the den, he cried with a lamentable voice unto Daniel: and the king spake and said to Daniel, O Daniel, servant of the living God, is thy God, whom thou servest continually, able to deliver thee from the lions?

Then said Daniel … O king, live for ever. My God hath sent his angel, and hath shut the lions' mouths, that they have not hurt me: forasmuch as before him innocency was found in me; and also before thee, O king, have I done no hurt.

Then was the king exceedingly glad for him, and commanded that they should take Daniel up out of the den. So Daniel was taken up out of the den, and no manner of hurt was found upon him, because he believed in his God.

… king commanded … those men which had accused Daniel … cast them into the den of lions …their children, and their wives; and the lions had the mastery of them, and brake all their bones in pieces or ever they came at the bottom of the den.

Then king Darius wrote unto all people, nations, and languages … Peace be multiplied unto you. I make a decree, That in every dominion of my kingdom men tremble and fear before the God of Daniel: for he is the living God, and stedfast for ever, and his kingdom that which shall not be destroyed, and his dominion shall be even unto the end.

17. Daniel Prayed for the Jewish Nation

Daniel 9:3-19; 10:10-14 KJV

And I set my face unto the Lord God, to seek by prayer and supplications, with fasting, and sackcloth, and ashes: And I prayed unto the LORD my God, and made my confession, and said, O Lord, the great and dreadful God, keeping the covenant and mercy to them that love him, and to them that keep his commandments;

We have sinned, and have committed iniquity, and have done wickedly, and have rebelled, even by departing from thy precepts and from thy judgments:

Neither have we hearkened unto thy servants the prophets, which spake in thy name to our kings, our princes, and our fathers, and to all the people of the land.

O LORD, righteousness belongeth unto thee, but unto us confusion of faces, as at this day; to the men of Judah, and to the inhabitants of Jerusalem, and unto all Israel, that are near, and that are far off, through all the countries whither thou hast driven them, because of their trespass that they have trespassed against thee.

O Lord, to us belongeth confusion of face, to our kings, to our princes, and to our fathers, because we have sinned against thee.

To the Lord our God belong mercies and forgivenesses, though we have rebelled against him; Neither have we obeyed the voice of the LORD our God, to walk in his laws, which he set before us by his servants the prophets.

Yea, all Israel have transgressed thy law, even by departing, that they might not obey thy voice; therefore the curse is poured upon us, and the oath that is written in the law of Moses the servant of God, because we have sinned against him.

And he hath confirmed his words, which he spake against us, and against our judges that judged us, by bringing upon us a great evil: for under the whole heaven hath not been done as hath been done upon Jerusalem ...

And now, O Lord our God, that hast brought thy people forth out of the land of Egypt with a mighty hand, and hast gotten thee renown, as at this day; we have sinned, we have done wickedly. O LORD, according to all thy righteousness, I beseech thee, let thine anger and thy fury be turned away from thy city Jerusalem, thy holy mountain: because for our sins, and for the iniquities of our fathers, Jerusalem and thy people are become a reproach to all that are about us.

Now therefore, O our God, hear the prayer of thy servant, and his supplications, and cause thy face to shine upon thy sanctuary that is desolate, for the Lord's sake.

O my God, incline thine ear, and hear; open thine eyes, and behold our desolations, and the city which is called by thy name: for we do not present our supplications before thee for our righteousnesses, but for thy great mercies.

O Lord, hear; O Lord, forgive; O Lord, hearken and do; defer not, for thine own sake, O my God: for thy city and thy people are called by thy name.

And, behold, an hand touched me, which set me upon my knees and upon the palms of my hands.

And he said unto me, O Daniel, a man greatly beloved, understand the words that I speak unto thee, and stand upright: for unto thee am I now sent. And when he had spoken this word unto me, I stood trembling.

Then said he unto me, Fear not, Daniel: for from the first day that thou didst set thine heart to understand, and to chasten thyself before thy God, thy words were heard, and I am come for thy words.

But the prince of the kingdom of Persia withstood me one and twenty days: but, lo, Michael, one of the chief princes, came to help me; and I remained there with the kings of Persia.

Now I am come to make thee understand what shall befall thy people in the latter days: for yet the vision is for many days.

18. David Prayer of Thanksgiving

2 Samuel 7:18-29 NIV

Then King David went in and sat before the Lord and prayed,

"Who am I, O Sovereign Lord, and what is my family, that you have brought me this far? And now, Sovereign Lord, in addition to everything else, you speak of giving your servant a lasting dynasty! Do you deal with everyone this way, O Sovereign Lord?

"What more can I say to you? You know what your servant is really like, Sovereign Lord. Because of your promise and according to your will, you have done all these great things and have made them known to your servant.

"How great you are, O Sovereign Lord! There is no one like you. We have never even heard of another God like you! What other nation on earth is like your people Israel? What other nation, O God, have you redeemed from slavery to be your own people? You made a great name for yourself when you redeemed your people from Egypt. You performed awesome miracles and drove out the nations and gods that stood in their way. You made Israel your very own people forever, and you, O Lord, became their God.

"And now, O Lord God, I am your servant; do as you have promised concerning me and my family. Confirm it as a promise that will last forever. And may your name be honored forever so that everyone will say, 'The Lord of Heaven's Armies is God over Israel!' And may the house of your servant David continue before you forever.

"O Lord of Heaven's Armies, God of Israel, I have been bold enough to pray this prayer to you because you have revealed all this to your servant, saying, 'I will build a house for you—a dynasty of kings!' For you are God, O Sovereign Lord. Your words are truth, and you have promised these good things to your servant. And now, may it please you to bless the house of your servant, so that it may continue forever before you. For you have spoken, and when you grant a blessing to your servant, O Sovereign Lord, it is an eternal blessing!"

19. David Prayed for Protection

Psalm 3 KJV

Lord, how are they increased that trouble me! many are they that rise up against me.

Many there be which say of my soul, There is no help for him in God. Selah.

But thou, O LORD, art a shield for me; my glory, and the lifter up of mine head.

I cried unto the LORD with my voice, and he heard me out of his holy hill. Selah.

I laid me down and slept; I awaked; for the LORD sustained me.

I will not be afraid of ten thousands of people, that have set themselves against me round about.

Arise, O LORD; save me, O my God: for thou hast smitten all mine enemies upon the cheek bone; thou hast broken the teeth of the ungodly.

Salvation belongeth unto the LORD: thy blessing is upon thy people. Selah.

Psalm 3 NIV

O LORD, how many are my foes!
How many rise up against me!
Many are saying of me,
"God will not deliver him." Selah [a]
But you are a shield around me, O LORD;
you bestow glory on me and lift [b] up my head.
To the LORD I cry aloud,
and he answers me from his holy hill. Selah
I lie down and sleep;
I wake again, because the LORD sustains me.

I will not fear the tens of thousands
drawn up against me on every side.
Arise, O LORD!
Deliver me, O my God! Strike all my enemies on the jaw;
break the teeth of the wicked.
From the LORD comes deliverance.
May your blessing be on your people. Selah

20. David Prepared for Building the Temple

1 Chronicles 29:1-19 NIV

Then King David said to the whole assembly: "My son Solomon, the one whom God has chosen, is young and inexperienced. The task is great, because this palatial structure is not for man but for the LORD God. With all my resources I have provided for the temple of my God—gold for the gold work, silver for the silver, bronze for the bronze, iron for the iron and wood for the wood, as well as onyx for the settings, turquoise, stones of various colors, and all kinds of fine stone and marble—all of these in large quantities. Besides, in my devotion to the temple of my God I now give my personal treasures of gold and silver for the temple of my God, over and above everything I have provided for this holy temple: three thousand talents£ of gold (gold of Ophir) and seven thousand talents£ of refined silver, for the overlaying of the walls of the buildings, for the gold work and the silver work, and for all the work to be done by the craftsmen. Now, who is willing to consecrate himself today to the LORD?"

Then the leaders of families, the officers of the tribes of Israel, the commanders of thousands and commanders of hundreds, and the officials in charge of the king's work gave willingly. They gave toward the work on the temple of God five thousand talents and ten thousand darics of gold, ten thousand talents£ of silver, eighteen thousand talents£ of bronze and a hundred thousand talents£ of iron. Any who had precious stones gave them to the treasury of the temple of the LORD in the custody of Jehiel the Gershonite. The people rejoiced at the willing response of their leaders, for they had given freely and wholeheartedly to the LORD. David the king also rejoiced greatly.

David praised the LORD in the presence of the whole assembly, saying,

"Praise be to you, O LORD,
God of our father Israel,
from everlasting to everlasting.
Yours, O LORD, is the greatness and the power
and the glory and the majesty and the splendor,
for everything in heaven and earth is yours.
Yours, O LORD, is the kingdom;
you are exalted as head over all.
Wealth and honor come from you;
you are the ruler of all things.
In your hands are strength and power
to exalt and give strength to all.
Now, our God, we give you thanks,
and praise your glorious name.

"But who am I, and who are my people, that we should be able to give as generously as this? Everything comes from you, and we have given you only what comes from your hand. We are aliens and strangers in your sight, as were all our forefathers. Our days on earth are like a shadow, without hope.

O LORD our God, as for all this abundance that we have provided for building you a temple for your Holy Name, it comes from your hand, and all of it belongs to you. I know, my God, that you test the heart and are pleased with integrity. All these things have I given willingly and with honest intent. And now I have seen with joy how willingly your people who are here have given to you.

O LORD, God of our fathers Abraham, Isaac and Israel, keep this desire in the hearts of your people forever, and keep their hearts loyal to you. And give my son Solomon the wholehearted devotion to keep your commands, requirements and decrees and to do everything to build the palatial structure for which I have provided."

21. David – An Evening Prayer

Psalm 4 KJV

Hear me when I call, O God of my righteousness: thou hast enlarged me when I was in distress; have mercy upon me, and hear my prayer.

O ye sons of men, how long will ye turn my glory into shame? how long will ye love vanity, and seek after leasing? Selah.

But know that the LORD hath set apart him that is godly for himself: the LORD will hear when I call unto him.

Stand in awe, and sin not: commune with your own heart upon your bed, and be still. Selah.

Offer the sacrifices of righteousness, and put your trust in the LORD.

There be many that say, Who will shew us any good? LORD, lift thou up the light of thy countenance upon us.

Thou hast put gladness in my heart, more than in the time that their corn and their wine increased.

I will both lay me down in peace, and sleep: for thou, LORD, only makest me dwell in safety.

22. David Prayed for Relief from Persecution

Psalm 7 KJV

O LORD my God, in thee do I put my trust: save me from all them that persecute me, and deliver me:

Lest he tear my soul like a lion, rending it in pieces, while there is none to deliver.

LORD my God, If I have done this; if there be iniquity in my hands;

If I have rewarded evil unto him that was at peace with me; (yea, I have delivered him that without cause is mine enemy:)

Let the enemy persecute my soul, and take it; yea, let him tread down my life upon the earth, and lay mine honour in the dust. Selah.

Arise, O LORD, in thine anger, lift up thyself because of the rage of mine enemies: and awake for me to the judgment that thou hast commanded.

So shall the congregation of the people compass thee about: for their sakes therefore return thou on high.

The LORD shall judge the people: judge me, O LORD, according to my righteousness, and according to mine integrity that is in me.

Oh let the wickedness of the wicked come to an end; but establish the just: for the righteous God trieth the hearts and reins.

My defence is of God, which saveth the upright in heart.

God judgeth the righteous, and God is angry with the wicked every day.

If he turn not, he will whet his sword; he hath bent his bow, and made it ready.

He hath also prepared for him the instruments of death; he ordaineth his arrows against the persecutors.

Behold, he travaileth with iniquity, and hath conceived mischief, and brought forth falsehood.

He made a pit, and digged it, and is fallen into the ditch which he made.

His mischief shall return upon his own head, and his violent dealing shall come down upon his own pate.

I will praise the LORD according to his righteousness: and will sing praise to the name of the LORD most high.

23. David Worshipped the Name of the Lord

Psalm 8 KJV

O LORD, our Lord, how excellent is thy name in all the earth! who hast set thy glory above the heavens.

Out of the mouth of babes and sucklings hast thou ordained strength because of thine enemies, that thou mightest still the enemy and the avenger.

When I consider thy heavens, the work of thy fingers, the moon and the stars, which thou hast ordained;

What is man, that thou art mindful of him? and the son of man, that thou visitest him?

For thou hast made him a little lower than the angels, and hast crowned him with glory and honour.

Thou madest him to have dominion over the works of thy hands; thou hast put all things under his feet:

All sheep and oxen, yea, and the beasts of the field;

The fowl of the air, and the fish of the sea, and whatsoever passeth through the paths of the seas.

O LORD our Lord, how excellent is thy name in all the earth!

24. David Prayed for Relief

Psalm 13 KJV

How long wilt thou forget me, O LORD? for ever? how long wilt thou hide thy face from me?

How long shall I take counsel in my soul, having sorrow in my heart daily? how long shall mine enemy be exalted over me?

Consider and hear me, O LORD my God: lighten mine eyes, lest I sleep the sleep of death;

Lest mine enemy say, I have prevailed against him; and those that trouble me rejoice when I am moved.

But I have trusted in thy mercy; my heart shall rejoice in thy salvation.

I will sing unto the LORD, because he hath dealt bountifully with me.

25. David – Psalm 23

Psalm 23 KJV

The LORD is my shepherd; I shall not want.

He maketh me to lie down in green pastures: he leadeth me beside the still waters.

He restoreth my soul: he leadeth me in the paths of righteousness for his name's sake.

Yea, though I walk through the valley of the shadow of death, I will fear no evil: for thou art with me; thy rod and thy staff they comfort me.

Thou preparest a table before me in the presence of mine enemies: thou anointest my head with oil; my cup runneth over.

Surely goodness and mercy shall follow me all the days of my life: and I will dwell in the house of the LORD for ever.

Psalm 23 NTL

The Lord is my shepherd;
I have all that I need.
He lets me rest in green meadows;
      he leads me beside peaceful streams.
He renews my strength.
He guides me along right paths,
      bringing honor to his name.
Even when I walk through the darkest valley,
I will not be afraid,
      for you are close beside me.
Your rod and your staff
      protect and comfort me.
You prepare a feast for me

in the presence of my enemies.
You honor me by anointing my head with oil.
My cup overflows with blessings.
Surely your goodness and unfailing love will pursue me
    all the days of my life, and I will live in the house of
the Lord
    forever.

26. David Prayed for God's Help

Psalm 25 KJV

O LORD my God, in thee do I put my trust: save me from all them that persecute me, and deliver me:

Lest he tear my soul like a lion, rending it in pieces, while there is none to deliver.

O LORD my God, If I have done this; if there be iniquity in my hands;

If I have rewarded evil unto him that was at peace with me; (yea, I have delivered him that without cause is mine enemy:)

Let the enemy persecute my soul, and take it; yea, let him tread down my life upon the earth, and lay mine honour in the dust. Selah.

Arise, O LORD, in thine anger, lift up thyself because of the rage of mine enemies: and awake for me to the judgment that thou hast commanded.

So shall the congregation of the people compass thee about: for their sakes therefore return thou on high.

The LORD shall judge the people: judge me, O LORD, according to my righteousness, and according to mine integrity that is in me.

Oh let the wickedness of the wicked come to an end; but establish the just: for the righteous God trieth the hearts and reins.

My defence is of God, which saveth the upright in heart.

God judgeth the righteous, and God is angry with the wicked every day.

If he turn not, he will whet his sword; he hath bent his bow, and made it ready.

He hath also prepared for him the instruments of death; he ordaineth his arrows against the persecutors.

Behold, he travaileth with iniquity, and hath conceived mischief, and brought forth falsehood.

He made a pit, and digged it, and is fallen into the ditch which he made.

His mischief shall return upon his own head, and his violent dealing shall come down upon his own pate.

I will praise the LORD according to his righteousness: and will sing praise to the name of the LORD most high.

27. David Prayed for Safety

Psalm 35 KJV

Plead my cause, O LORD, with them that strive with me: fight against them that fight against me. Take hold of shield and buckler, and stand up for mine help.

Draw out also the spear, and stop the way against them that persecute me: say unto my soul, I am thy salvation. Let them be confounded and put to shame that seek after my soul: let them be turned back and brought to confusion that devise my hurt.

Let them be as chaff before the wind: and let the angel of the LORD chase them ... their way be dark and slippery: and let the angel of the LORD persecute them.

For without cause have they hid for me their net in a pit, which without cause they have digged for my soul. Let destruction come upon him at unawares; and let his net that he hath hid catch himself: into that very destruction let him fall.

And my soul shall be joyful in the LORD: it shall rejoice in his salvation.

All my bones shall say, LORD, who is like unto thee, which deliverest the poor from him that is too strong for him, yea, the poor and the needy from him that spoileth him? False witnesses did rise up; they laid to my charge things ...

They rewarded me evil for good to the spoiling of my soul.

But as for me, when they were sick, my clothing was sackcloth: I humbled my soul with fasting; and my prayer returned into mine own bosom.

I behaved myself as though he had been my friend or brother: I bowed down heavily, as one that mourneth for his mother. But in mine adversity they rejoiced, and gathered themselves together: yea, the abjects gathered themselves together against me, and I knew it not; they did tear me, and ceased not:

With hypocritical mockers in feasts, they gnashed upon me with their teeth.

Lord, how long wilt thou look on? rescue my soul from their destructions, my darling from the lions. I will give thee thanks in the great congregation: I will praise thee among much people. Let not them that are mine enemies wrongfully rejoice over me: neither let them wink with the eye that hate me without a cause.

For they speak not peace: but they devise deceitful matters against them that are quiet in the land. Yea, they opened their mouth wide against me, and said, Aha, aha, our eye hath seen it. ... O LORD: keep not silence: O Lord, be not far from me. Stir up thyself, and awake to my judgment, even unto my cause, my God and my Lord.

Judge me, O LORD my God, according to thy righteousness; and let them not rejoice over me. Let them not say in their hearts, Ah, so would we have it: let them not say, We have swallowed him up.

Let them be ashamed and brought to confusion together that rejoice at mine hurt ... be clothed with shame and dishonour that magnify themselves against me ... shout for joy ... be glad, that favour my righteous cause: ... let them say continually, Let the LORD be magnified, which hath pleasure in the prosperity of his servant. ... my tongue shall speak of thy righteousness ... thy praise all the day long.

28. David Sought Forgiveness of His Sin

Psalm 51

Have mercy upon me, O God, according to thy lovingkindness: according unto the multitude of thy tender mercies blot out my transgressions.

Wash me throughly from mine iniquity, and cleanse me from my sin. For I acknowledge my transgressions: and my sin is ever before me.

Against thee, thee only, have I sinned, and done this evil in thy sight: that thou mightest be justified when thou speakest, and be clear when thou judgest.

Behold, I was shapen in iniquity; and in sin did my mother conceive me.

Behold, thou desirest truth in the inward parts: and in the hidden part thou shalt make me to know wisdom.

Purge me with hyssop, and I shall be clean: wash me, and I shall be whiter than snow. Make me to hear joy and gladness; that the bones which thou hast broken may rejoice.

Hide thy face from my sins, and blot out all mine iniquities. Create in me a clean heart, O God; and renew a right spirit within me.

Cast me not away from thy presence; and take not thy holy spirit from me. Restore unto me the joy of thy salvation; and uphold me with thy free spirit.

Then will I teach transgressors thy ways; and sinners shall be converted unto thee.

Deliver me from bloodguiltiness, O God, thou God of my salvation: and my tongue shall sing aloud of thy righteousness.

O Lord, open thou my lips; and my mouth shall shew forth thy praise. For thou desirest not sacrifice; else would I give it: thou delightest not in burnt offering.

The sacrifices of God are a broken spirit: a broken and a contrite heart, O God, thou wilt not despise. Do good in thy good pleasure unto Zion: build thou the walls of Jerusalem.

Then shalt thou be pleased with the sacrifices of righteousness, with burnt offering and whole burnt offering: then shall they offer bullocks upon thine altar.

29. David Praised the Lord

Psalm 150 KJV

Praise ye the LORD. Praise God in his sanctuary: praise him in the firmament of his power.

Praise him for his mighty acts: praise him according to his excellent greatness.

Praise him with the sound of the trumpet: praise him with the psaltery and harp.

Praise him with the timbrel and dance: praise him with stringed instruments and organs.

Praise him upon the loud cymbals: praise him upon the high sounding cymbals.

Let every thing that hath breath praise the LORD. Praise ye the LORD.

30. Elijah Prayed To Raise The Widow's Son

1 Kings 17:17-24 KJV

And it came to pass after these things, that the son of the woman, the mistress of the house, fell sick; and his sickness was so sore, that there was no breath left in him.

And she said unto Elijah, What have I to do with thee, O thou man of God? art thou come unto me to call my sin to remembrance, and to slay my son?

And he said unto her, Give me thy son. And he took him out of her bosom, and carried him up into a loft, where he abode, and laid him upon his own bed.

And he cried unto the LORD, and said, O LORD my God, hast thou also brought evil upon the widow with whom I sojourn, by slaying her son?

And he stretched himself upon the child three times, and cried unto the LORD, and said, O LORD my God, I pray thee, let this child's soul come into him again.

And the LORD heard the voice of Elijah; and the soul of the child came into him again, and he revived.

And Elijah took the child, and brought him down out of the chamber into the house, and delivered him unto his mother: and Elijah said, See, thy son liveth.

And the woman said to Elijah, Now by this I know that thou art a man of God, and that the word of the LORD in thy mouth is truth.

31. Elijah Prayed For Triumph over Baal

1 Kings 18:36-38

And it came to pass at the time of the offering of the evening sacrifice, that Elijah the prophet came near, and said, LORD God of Abraham, Isaac, and of Israel, let it be known this day that thou art God in Israel, and that I am thy servant, and that I have done all these things at thy word.

Hear me, O LORD, hear me, that this people may know that thou art the LORD God, and that thou hast turned their heart back again.

Then the fire of the LORD fell, and consumed the burnt sacrifice, and the wood, and the stones, and the dust, and licked up the water that was in the trench.

32. Elijah Prayed For Rain

James 5:17 AMP

Elijah was a human being with a nature such as we have [with feelings, affections, and a constitution like ours]; and he prayed earnestly for it not to rain, and no rain fell on the earth for three years and six months.

And [then] he prayed again and the heavens supplied rain and the land produced its crops [as usual].

33. Elijah Prayed to Die

1 Kings 19:1-8 KJV

And Ahab told Jezebel all that Elijah had done, and withal how he had slain all the prophets with the sword.

Then Jezebel sent a messenger unto Elijah, saying, So let the gods do to me, and more also, if I make not thy life as the life of one of them by to morrow about this time.

And when he saw that, he arose, and went for his life, and came to Beersheba, which belongeth to Judah, and left his servant there.

But he himself went a day's journey into the wilderness, and came and sat down under a juniper tree: and he requested for himself that he might die; and said, It is enough; now, O LORD, take away my life; for I am not better than my fathers.

And as he lay and slept under a juniper tree, behold, then an angel touched him, and said unto him, Arise and eat.

And he looked, and, behold, there was a cake baken on the coals, and a cruse of water at his head. And he did eat and drink, and laid him down again.

And the angel of the LORD came again the second time, and touched him, and said, Arise and eat; because the journey is too great for thee.

And he arose, and did eat and drink, and went in the strength of that meat forty days and forty nights unto Horeb the mount of God.

34. Elisha Prayed for Victory

2 Kings 6:8-23

Then the king of Syria warred against Israel, and took counsel with his servants, saying, In such and such a place shall be my camp.

And the man of God sent unto the king of Israel, saying, Beware that thou pass not such a place; for thither the Syrians are come down.

And the king of Israel sent to the place which the man of God told him and warned him of, and saved himself there, not once nor twice.

Therefore the heart of the king of Syria was sore troubled for this thing; and he called his servants, and said unto them, Will ye not shew me which of us is for the king of Israel? And one of his servants said, None, my lord, O king: but Elisha, the prophet that is in Israel, telleth the king of Israel the words that thou speakest in thy bedchamber. And he said, Go and spy where he is, that I may send and fetch him. And it was told him, saying, Behold, he is in Dothan. Therefore sent he thither horses, and chariots, and a great host: and they came by night, and compassed the city about.

And when the servant of the man of God was risen early, and gone forth, behold, an host compassed the city both with horses and chariots. And his servant said unto him, Alas, my master! how shall we do? And he answered, Fear not: for they that be with us are more than they that be with them.

And Elisha prayed ... LORD, I pray thee, open his eyes, that he may see. And the LORD opened the eyes of the young man; and he saw: and, behold, the mountain was full of horses and chariots of fire round about Elisha.

... Elisha prayed unto the LORD ... Smite this people, I pray thee, with blindness. And he smote them with blindness according to the word of Elisha.

And Elisha said ... This is not the way, neither is this the city: follow me, and I will bring you to the man whom ye seek. But he led them to Samaria. And it came to pass, when they were come into Samaria, that Elisha said, LORD, open the eyes of these men, that they may see. And the LORD opened their eyes, and they saw; and, behold, they were in the midst of Samaria.

... the king of Israel said unto Elisha ... My father, shall I smite them ...

And he answered, Thou shalt not smite them: wouldest thou smite those whom thou hast taken captive with thy sword and with thy bow? set bread and water before them, that they may eat and drink, and go to their master.

And he prepared great provision for them: and when they had eaten and drunk, he sent them away, and they went to their master. So the bands of Syria came no more into the land of Israel.

35. Esther & Mordecai Fast for Israel

Esther 3:8-10, 4:7-16 KJV

And Haman said unto king Ahasuerus, There is a certain people scattered abroad and dispersed among the people in all the provinces of thy kingdom; and their laws are diverse from all people; neither keep they the king's laws: therefore it is not for the king's profit to suffer them. If it please the king, let it be written that they may be destroyed: and I will pay ten thousand talents of silver to the hands of those that have the charge of the business, to bring it into the king's treasuries. And the king took his ring from his hand, and gave it unto Haman the son of Hammedatha the Agagite, the Jews' enemy ...

And Mordecai told him of all that had happened unto him, and of the sum of the money that Haman had promised to pay to the king's treasuries for the Jews, to destroy them. Also he gave him the copy of the writing of the decree that was given at Shushan to destroy them, to shew it unto Esther, and to declare it unto her, and to charge her that she should go in unto the king, to make supplication unto him, and to make request before him for her people.

And Hatach came and told Esther the words of Mordecai.

Again Esther spake unto Hatach, and gave him commandment unto Mordecai; All the king's servants, and the people of the king's provinces, do know, that whosoever, whether man or women, shall come unto the king into the inner court, who is not called, there is one law of his to put him to death, except such to whom the king shall hold out the golden sceptre, that he may live: but I have not been called to come in unto the king these thirty days.

And they told to Mordecai Esther's words.

Then Mordecai commanded to answer Esther, Think not with thyself that thou shalt escape in the king's house, more than all the Jews. For if thou altogether holdest thy peace at this time, then shall there enlargement and deliverance arise to the Jews from another place; but thou and thy father's house shall be destroyed: and who knoweth whether thou art come to the kingdom for such a time as this?

Then Esther bade them return Mordecai this answer, Go, gather together all the Jews that are present in Shushan, and fast ye for me, and neither eat nor drink three days, night or day: I also and my maidens will fast likewise; and so will I go in unto the king, which is not according to the law: and if I perish, I perish.

36. Ezra Prayed - Fasted for Protection

Ezra 8:21-23 KJV

Then I proclaimed a fast there, at the river of Ahava, that we might afflict ourselves before our God, to seek of him a right way for us, and for our little ones, and for all our substance. For I was ashamed to require of the king a band of soldiers and horsemen to help us against the enemy in the way: because we had spoken unto the king, saying, The hand of our God is upon all them for good that seek him; but his power and his wrath is against all them that forsake him.

So we fasted and besought our God for this: and he was intreated of us.

37. Ezra Prayed For the Sins of the People

Ezra 9:6-15 KJV

And said, O my God, I am ashamed and blush to lift up my face to thee, my God: for our iniquities are increased over our head, and our trespass is grown up unto the heavens. Since the days of our fathers have we been in a great trespass unto this day; and for our iniquities have we, our kings, and our priests, been delivered into the hand of the kings of the lands, to the sword, to captivity, and to a spoil, and to confusion of face … now for a little space grace hath been shewed from the LORD our God, to leave us a remnant to escape, and to give us a nail in his holy place, that our God may lighten our eyes, and give us a little reviving in our bondage.

For we were bondmen; yet our God hath not forsaken us in our bondage, but hath extended mercy unto us in the sight of the kings of Persia, to give us a reviving, to set up the house of our God, and to repair the desolations thereof, and to give us a wall in Judah and in Jerusalem.

And now, O our God, what shall we say after this? for we have forsaken thy commandments, Which thou hast commanded by thy servants the prophets, saying, The land, unto which ye go to possess it, is an unclean land with the filthiness of the people of the lands, with their abominations, which have filled it from one end to another with their uncleanness.

Now therefore give not your daughters unto their sons, neither take their daughters unto your sons, nor seek their peace or their wealth for ever: that ye may be strong, and eat the good of the land, and leave it for an inheritance to your children for ever. And after all that is come upon us for our evil deeds, and for our great trespass, seeing that thou our God hast punished us less than our iniquities deserve, and hast given us such deliverance as this; Should we again break thy commandments, and join in affinity with the people of these abominations? wouldest not thou be angry with us till thou hadst consumed us, so that there should be no remnant nor escaping?

O LORD God of Israel, thou art righteous: for we remain yet escaped, as it is this day: behold, we are before thee in our trespasses: for we cannot stand before thee because of this.

38. Father Asked for Help for Son and Help with His Unbelief

Matthew 17:15; Mark 9:17-27 KJV

Lord, have mercy on my son: for he is lunatick, and sore vexed: for ofttimes he falleth into the fire, and oft into the water.

And one of the multitude answered and said, Master, I have brought unto thee my son, which hath a dumb spirit;

And wheresoever he taketh him, he teareth him: and he foameth, and gnasheth with his teeth, and pineth away: and I spake to thy disciples that they should cast him out; and they could not.

He answereth him, and saith, O faithless generation, how long shall I be with you? how long shall I suffer you? bring him unto me.

And they brought him unto him: and when he saw him, straightway the spirit tare him; and he fell on the ground, and wallowed foaming.

And he asked his father, How long is it ago since this came unto him? And he said, Of a child.

And ofttimes it hath cast him into the fire, and into the waters, to destroy him: but if thou canst do any thing, have compassion on us, and help us.

Jesus said unto him, If thou canst believe, all things are possible to him that believeth.

And straightway the father of the child cried out, and said with tears, Lord, I believe; help thou mine unbelief.

When Jesus saw that the people came running together, he rebuked the foul spirit, saying unto him, Thou dumb and deaf spirit, I charge thee, come out of him, and enter no more into him.

And the spirit cried, and rent him sore, and came out of him: and he was as one dead; insomuch that many said, He is dead.

But Jesus took him by the hand, and lifted him up; and he arose.

39. Gideon Asked God for Proof of His Call - Twice

Judges 6:12-17, 36-40 KJV

And the angel of the LORD appeared unto him, and said unto him, The LORD is with thee, thou mighty man of valour.

And Gideon said unto him, Oh my Lord, if the LORD be with us, why then is all this befallen us? and where be all his miracles which our fathers told us of, saying, Did not the LORD bring us up from Egypt? but now the LORD hath forsaken us, and delivered us into the hands of the Midianites.

And the LORD looked upon him, and said, Go in this thy might, and thou shalt save Israel from the hand of the Midianites: have not I sent thee?

And he said unto him, Oh my Lord, wherewith shall I save Israel? behold, my family is poor in Manasseh, and I am the least in my father's house.

And the LORD said unto him, Surely I will be with thee, and thou shalt smite the Midianites as one man.

And he said unto him, If now I have found grace in thy sight, then shew me a sign that thou talkest with me …

… And Gideon said unto God, If thou wilt save Israel by mine hand, as thou hast said,

Behold, I will put a fleece of wool in the floor; and if the dew be on the fleece only, and it be dry upon all the earth beside, then shall I know that thou wilt save Israel by mine hand, as thou hast said.

And it was so: for he rose up early on the morrow, and thrust the fleece together, and wringed the dew out of the fleece, a bowl full of water.

And Gideon said unto God, Let not thine anger be hot against me, and I will speak but this once: let me prove, I pray thee, but this once with the fleece; let it now be dry only upon the fleece, and upon all the ground let there be dew.

And God did so that night: for it was dry upon the fleece only, and there was dew on all the ground.

40. Habakkuk Prayed for Revival in Shigionoth

Habakkuk 3:2-19 KJV

O LORD, I have heard thy speech, and was afraid: O LORD, revive thy work in the midst of the years, in the midst of the years make known; in wrath remember mercy. God came from Teman, and the Holy One from mount Paran. Selah. His glory covered the heavens, and the earth was full of his praise. And his brightness was as the light; he had horns coming out of his hand: and there was the hiding of his power.

Before him went the pestilence, and burning coals went forth at his feet. He stood, and measured the earth: he beheld, and drove asunder the nations; and the everlasting mountains were scattered, the perpetual hills did bow: his ways are everlasting.

I saw the tents of Cushan in affliction: and the curtains of the land of Midian did tremble. Was the LORD displeased against the rivers? was thine anger against the rivers? was thy wrath against the sea, that thou didst ride upon thine horses and thy chariots of salvation?

Thy bow was made quite naked, according to the oaths of the tribes, even thy word. Selah. Thou didst cleave the earth with rivers.

The mountains saw thee, and they trembled: the overflowing of the water passed by: the deep uttered his voice, and lifted up his hands on high. The sun and moon stood still in their habitation: at the light of thine arrows they went, and at the shining of thy glittering spear.

Thou didst march through the land in indignation, thou didst thresh the heathen in anger. Thou wentest forth for the salvation of thy people, even for salvation with thine anointed; thou woundedst the head out of the house of the wicked, by discovering the foundation unto the neck. Selah.

Thou didst strike through with his staves the head of his villages: they came out as a whirlwind to scatter me: their rejoicing was as to devour the poor secretly. Thou didst walk through the sea with thine horses, through the heap of great waters.

When I heard, my belly trembled; my lips quivered at the voice: rottenness entered into my bones, and I trembled in myself, that I might rest in the day of trouble: when he cometh up unto the people, he will invade them with his troops.

Although the fig tree shall not blossom, neither shall fruit be in the vines; the labour of the olive shall fail, and the fields shall yield no meat; the flock shall be cut off from the fold, and there shall be no herd in the stalls: Yet I will rejoice in the LORD, I will joy in the God of my salvation.

The LORD God is my strength, and he will make my feet like hinds' feet, and he will make me to walk upon mine high places. To the chief singer on my stringed instruments.

41. Hannah Prayed for a Son

1 Samuel 1:9-28 KJV

So Hannah rose up after they had eaten in Shiloh, and after they had drunk. Now Eli the priest sat upon a seat by a post of the temple of the LORD.

And she was in bitterness of soul, and prayed unto the LORD, and wept sore. And she vowed a vow, and said, O LORD of hosts, if thou wilt indeed look on the affliction of thine handmaid, and remember me, and not forget thine handmaid, but wilt give unto thine handmaid a man child, then I will give him unto the LORD all the days of his life, and there shall no razor come upon his head.

... she continued praying before the LORD, that Eli marked her mouth.

Now Hannah, she spake in her heart; only her lips moved, but her voice was not heard: therefore Eli thought she had been drunken.

And Eli said ... How long wilt thou be drunken? put away thy wine from thee.

... Hannah answered ... No, my lord, I am a woman of a sorrowful spirit: I have drunk neither wine nor strong drink, but have poured out my soul before the LORD.

Count not thine handmaid for a daughter of Belial: for out of the abundance of my complaint and grief have I spoken hitherto. Then Eli answered and said, Go in peace: and the God of Israel grant thee thy petition that thou hast asked of him.

And she said, Let thine handmaid find grace in thy sight. So the woman went her way, and did eat, and her countenance was no more sad. And they rose up in the morning early, and worshipped before the LORD, and returned, and came to their house to Ramah: and Elkanah knew Hannah his wife; and the LORD remembered her. ... when the time was come about after Hannah had conceived, that she bare a son, and called his name Samuel, saying, Because I have asked him of the LORD.

And the man Elkanah, and all his house, went up to offer unto the LORD the yearly sacrifice, and his vow. But Hannah went not up; for she said unto her husband, I will not go up until the child be weaned, and then I will bring him, that he may appear before the LORD, and there abide for ever.

And Elkanah her husband said unto her, Do what seemeth thee good; tarry until thou have weaned him; only the LORD establish his word. So the woman abode, and gave her son suck until she weaned him. And when she had weaned him, she took him up with her, with three bullocks, and one ephah of flour, and a bottle of wine, and brought him unto the house of the LORD in Shiloh: and the child was young.

And they slew a bullock, and brought the child to Eli. And she said, Oh my lord, as thy soul liveth, my lord, I am the woman that stood by thee here, praying unto the LORD. For this child I prayed; and the LORD hath given me my petition which I asked of him:

Therefore also I have lent him to the LORD; as long as he liveth he shall be lent to the LORD. And he worshipped the LORD there.

42. Hannah's Prayer of Thanksgiving

1 Samuel 2:1-11 KJV

And Hannah prayed, and said, My heart rejoiceth in the LORD, mine horn is exalted in the LORD: my mouth is enlarged over mine enemies; because I rejoice in thy salvation.

There is none holy as the LORD: for there is none beside thee: neither is there any rock like our God.

Talk no more so exceeding proudly; let not arrogancy come out of your mouth: for the LORD is a God of knowledge, and by him actions are weighed.

The bows of the mighty men are broken, and they that stumbled are girded with strength.

They that were full have hired out themselves for bread; and they that were hungry ceased: so that the barren hath born seven; and she that hath many children is waxed feeble.

The LORD killeth, and maketh alive: he bringeth down to the grave, and bringeth up.

The LORD maketh poor, and maketh rich: he bringeth low, and lifteth up.

He raiseth up the poor out of the dust, and lifteth up the beggar from the dunghill, to set them among princes, and to make them inherit the throne of glory: for the pillars of the earth are the LORD's, and he hath set the world upon them.

He will keep the feet of his saints, and the wicked shall be silent in darkness; for by strength shall no man prevail.

The adversaries of the LORD shall be broken to pieces; out of heaven shall he thunder upon them: the LORD shall judge the ends of the earth; and he shall give strength unto his king, and exalt the horn of his anointed.

And Elkanah went to Ramah to his house. And the child did minister unto the LORD before Eli the priest.

43. Hezekiah Prayed for Victory

2 Kings 19:9-10, 14-19, 20-22, 34-35 NIV

Now Sennacherib received a report that Tirhakah, the Cushite [a] king of Egypt , was marching out to fight against him. So he again sent messengers to Hezekiah with this word: "Say to Hezekiah king of Judah: Do not let the god you depend on deceive you when he says, 'Jerusalem will not be handed over to the king of Assyria.' ...

Hezekiah received the letter from the messengers and read it. Then he went up to the temple of the LORD and spread it out before the LORD. And Hezekiah prayed to the LORD : "O LORD, God of Israel, enthroned between the cherubim, you alone are God over all the kingdoms of the earth. You have made heaven and earth. Give ear, O LORD, and hear; open your eyes, O LORD, and see; listen to the words Sennacherib has sent to insult the living God.

"It is true, O LORD, that the Assyrian kings have laid waste these nations and their lands. They have thrown their gods into the fire and destroyed them, for they were not gods but only wood and stone, fashioned by men's hands. Now, O LORD our God, deliver us from his hand, so that all kingdoms on earth may know that you alone, O LORD, are God."

Then Isaiah son of Amoz sent a message to Hezekiah: "This is what the LORD, the God of Israel, says: I have heard your prayer concerning Sennacherib king of Assyria. This is the word that the LORD has spoken against him:

"'The Virgin Daughter of Zion despises you and mocks you. The Daughter of Jerusalem tosses her head as you flee. Who is it you have insulted and blasphemed?

Against whom have you raised your voice and lifted your eyes in pride? Against the Holy One of Israel! I will defend this city and save it, for my sake and for the sake of David my servant."

That night the angel of the LORD went out and put to death a hundred and eighty-five thousand men in the Assyrian camp. When the people got up the next morning—there were all the dead bodies!

44. Hezekiah Prayed for Health

2 Kings 20:1-11 KJV

In those days was Hezekiah sick unto death. And the prophet Isaiah the son of Amoz came to him, and said unto him, Thus saith the LORD, Set thine house in order; for thou shalt die, and not live.

Then he turned his face to the wall, and prayed unto the LORD, saying,

I beseech thee, O LORD, remember now how I have walked before thee in truth and with a perfect heart, and have done that which is good in thy sight. And Hezekiah wept sore.

And it came to pass, afore Isaiah was gone out into the middle court, that the word of the LORD came to him, saying,

Turn again, and tell Hezekiah the captain of my people, Thus saith the LORD, the God of David thy father, I have heard thy prayer, I have seen thy tears: behold, I will heal thee: on the third day thou shalt go up unto the house of the LORD.

And I will add unto thy days fifteen years; and I will deliver thee and this city out of the hand of the king of Assyria; and I will defend this city for mine own sake, and for my servant David's sake.

And Isaiah said, Take a lump of figs. And they took and laid it on the boil, and he recovered.

And Hezekiah said unto Isaiah, What shall be the sign that the LORD will heal me, and that I shall go up into the house of the LORD the third day?

And Isaiah said, This sign shalt thou have of the LORD, that the LORD will do the thing that he hath spoken: shall the shadow go forward ten degrees, or go back ten degrees?

And Hezekiah answered, It is a light thing for the shadow to go down ten degrees: nay, but let the shadow return backward ten degrees.

And Isaiah the prophet cried unto the LORD: and he brought the shadow ten degrees backward, by which it had gone down in the dial of Ahaz.

45. Hezekiah's Prayer for Safety from Assyria

Isaiah 37:14-35 KJV

And Hezekiah received the letter of the hand of the messengers ... and Hezekiah went up into the house of the LORD, and spread it before the LORD ... Hezekiah prayed ... O LORD God of Israel, which dwellest between the cherubims, thou art the God, even thou alone, of all the kingdoms of the earth; thou hast made heaven and earth. LORD, bow down thine ear, and hear:

open, LORD, thine eyes, and see: and hear the words of Sennacherib, which hath sent him to reproach the living God.

Of a truth, LORD, the kings of Assyria have destroyed the nations and their lands, And have cast their gods into the fire: for they were no gods, but the work of men's hands, wood and stone ... I beseech thee, save thou us out of his hand, that all the kingdoms of the earth may know that thou art the LORD God ...

Then Isaiah the son of Amoz sent to Hezekiah, saying, Thus saith the LORD God of Israel, That which thou hast prayed to me against Sennacherib king of Assyria I have heard ... The virgin the daughter of Zion hath despised thee, and laughed thee to scorn; the daughter of Jerusalem hath shaken her head at thee. Whom hast thou reproached and blasphemed? and against whom hast thou exalted thy voice, and lifted up thine eyes on high? even against the Holy One of Israel.

By thy messengers thou hast reproached the LORD, and hast said, With the multitude of my chariots I am come up to the height of the mountains, to the sides of Lebanon, and will cut down the tall cedar trees ... the choice fir trees thereof: and I will enter into the lodgings of his borders, and into the forest of his Carmel.

I have digged and drunk strange waters, and with the sole of my feet have I dried up all the rivers of besieged places. Hast thou not heard long ago how I have done it, and of ancient times that I have formed it? now have I brought it to pass, that thou shouldest be to lay waste fenced cities into ruinous heaps ... their inhabitants were of small power ... dismayed and confounded; they were as the grass of the field ... as the green herb, as the grass on the house tops, and as corn blasted before it be grown up.

But I know thy abode, and thy going out, and thy coming in, and thy rage against me. Because thy rage against me and thy tumult is come up into mine ears, therefore I will put my hook in thy nose, and my bridle in thy lips, and I will turn thee back by the way by which thou camest. And this shall be a sign unto thee, Ye shall eat this year such things as grow of themselves, and in the second year that which springeth of the same; and in the third year sow ye, and reap, and plant vineyards, and eat the fruits thereof.

And the remnant that is escaped of the house of Judah shall yet again take root downward, and bear fruit upward. For out of Jerusalem shall go forth a remnant, and they that escape out of mount Zion: the zeal of the LORD of hosts shall do this.

... thus saith the LORD concerning the king of Assyria, He shall not come into this city, nor shoot an arrow there, nor come before it with shield, nor cast a bank against it. By the way that he came, by the same shall he return, and shall not come into this city, saith the LORD. For I will defend this city ...

46. Isaac Prayed for Rebekah to Conceive

Genesis 25:21-26 KJV

And Isaac intreated the LORD for his wife, because she was barren: and the LORD was intreated of him, and Rebekah his wife conceived.

And the children struggled together within her; and she said, If it be so, why am I thus? And she went to enquire of the LORD.

And the LORD said unto her, Two nations are in thy womb, and two manner of people shall be separated from thy bowels; and the one people shall be stronger than the other people; and the elder shall serve the younger.

And when her days to be delivered were fulfilled, behold, there were twins in her womb.

And the first came out red, all over like an hairy garment; and they called his name Esau.

And after that came his brother out, and his hand took hold on Esau's heel; and his name was called Jacob: and Isaac was threescore years old when she bare them.

And the boys grew: and Esau was a cunning hunter, a man of the field; and Jacob was a plain man, dwelling in tents.

47. Isaiah Prayed for Mercy and Pardon for Israel

Isaiah 63:15-19 CEV

> Lord, look down from heaven;
> > look from your holy, glorious home, and see us.
> Where is the passion and the might
> > you used to show on our behalf?
> Where are your mercy and compassion now?
> Surely you are still our Father!
> Even if Abraham and Jacob would disown us,
> Lord, you would still be our Father.
> You are our Redeemer from ages past.
> Lord, why have you allowed us to turn from your path?
> Why have you given us stubborn hearts so we no longer
> fear you?
> > Return and help us, for we are your servants,
> > > the tribes that are your special possession.
> How briefly your holy people possessed your holy place,
> > and now our enemies have destroyed it.
> Sometimes it seems as though we never belonged to you,
> > as though we had never been known as your people.

48. Jabez Prayer to the Lord for Blessings

1 Chronicles 4:9-10

KJV

And Jabez was more honourable than his brethren: and his mother called his name Jabez, saying, Because I bare him with sorrow.

And Jabez called on the God of Israel, saying, Oh that thou wouldest bless me indeed, and enlarge my coast, and that thine hand might be with me, and that thou wouldest keep me from evil, that it may not grieve me! And God granted him that which he requested.

NLT

There was a man named Jabez who was more honorable than any of his brothers. His mother named him Jabez because his birth had been so painful. He was the one who prayed to the God of Israel, "Oh, that you would bless me and expand my territory! Please be with me in all that I do, and keep me from all trouble and pain!" And God granted him his request.

AMP

Jabez was honorable above his brothers; but his mother named him Jabez [sorrow maker], saying, Because I bore him in pain.

Jabez cried to the God of Israel, saying, Oh, that You would bless me and enlarge my border, and that Your hand might be with me, and You would keep me from evil so it might not hurt me! And God granted his request.

CEV

Jabez was a man who got his name because of the pain he caused his mother during birth. But he was still the most respected son in his family. One day he prayed to Israel's God, "Please bless me and give me a lot of land. Be with me so I will be safe from harm." And God did just what Jabez had asked.

49. Jacob Prayed for Deliverance From His Brother Esau

Genesis 32:9-12 KJV

And Jacob said, O God of my father Abraham, and God of my father Isaac, the LORD which saidst unto me, Return unto thy country, and to thy kindred, and I will deal well with thee:

I am not worthy of the least of all the mercies, and of all the truth, which thou hast shewed unto thy servant; for with my staff I passed over this Jordan; and now I am become two bands.

Deliver me, I pray thee, from the hand of my brother, from the hand of Esau: for I fear him, lest he will come and smite me, and the mother with the children.

And thou saidst, I will surely do thee good, and make thy seed as the sand of the sea, which cannot be numbered for multitude.

50. Jacob Wrestled With an Angel

Genesis 32:24-30 KJV

And Jacob was left alone; and there wrestled a man with him until the breaking of the day.

And when he saw that he prevailed not against him, he touched the hollow of his thigh; and the hollow of Jacob's thigh was out of joint, as he wrestled with him.

And he said, Let me go, for the day breaketh. And he said, I will not let thee go, except thou bless me.

And he said unto him, What is thy name? And he said, Jacob.

And he said, Thy name shall be called no more Jacob, but Israel: for as a prince hast thou power with God and with men, and hast prevailed.

And Jacob asked him, and said, Tell me, I pray thee, thy name. And he said, Wherefore is it that thou dost ask after my name? And he blessed him there.

And Jacob called the name of the place Peniel: for I have seen God face to face, and my life is preserved.

And as he passed over Penuel the sun rose upon him, and he halted upon his thigh.

Therefore the children of Israel eat not of the sinew which shrank, which is upon the hollow of the thigh, unto this day:

because he touched the hollow of Jacob's thigh in the sinew that shrank.

51. Jehoshaphat Sought Judah's Protection

2 Chronicles 20:2-3, 5-12, 17-18, 22, 24 KJV

Then there came some that told Jehoshaphat, saying, There cometh a great multitude against thee from beyond the sea on this side Syria; and, behold, they be in Hazazontamar, which is Engedi.

And Jehoshaphat feared, and set himself to seek the LORD, and proclaimed a fast throughout all Judah ... [he] stood in the congregation of Judah and Jerusalem, in the house of the LORD, before the new court, And said, O LORD God of our fathers, art not thou God in heaven? and rulest not thou over all the kingdoms of the heathen? and in thine hand is there not power and might, so that none is able to withstand thee?

Art not thou our God, who didst drive out the inhabitants of this land before thy people Israel, and gavest it to the seed of Abraham thy friend for ever? And they dwelt therein, and have built thee a sanctuary therein for thy name, saying,

If, when evil cometh upon us, as the sword, judgment, or pestilence, or famine, we stand before this house, and in thy presence, (for thy name is in this house,) and cry unto thee in our affliction, then thou wilt hear and help ... the children of Ammon and Moab and mount Seir, whom thou wouldest not let Israel invade, when they came out of the land of Egypt, but they turned from them, and destroyed them not;

Behold, I say, how they reward us, to come to cast us out of thy possession, which thou hast given us to inherit. O our God, wilt thou not judge them? for we have no might against this great company that cometh against us; neither know we what to do: but our eyes are upon thee...

Ye shall not need to fight in this battle: set yourselves, stand ye still, and see the salvation of the LORD with you, O Judah and Jerusalem: fear not, nor be dismayed; to morrow go out against them: for the LORD will be with you.

And Jehoshaphat bowed his head with his face to the ground: and all Judah and the inhabitants of Jerusalem fell before the LORD, worshipping the LORD ... when they began to sing and to praise, the LORD set ambushments against the children of Ammon, Moab, and mount Seir, which were come against Judah; and they were smitten.

And when Judah came toward the watch tower in the wilderness, they looked unto the multitude, and, behold, they were dead bodies fallen to the earth, and none escaped.

52. Jeremiah Prayed for God's Patience

Jeremiah 14:7:22 KJV

O LORD, though our iniquities testify against us, do thou it for thy name's sake: for our backslidings are many; we have sinned against thee. O the hope of Israel, the saviour thereof in time of trouble, why shouldest thou be as a stranger in the land, and as a wayfaring man that turneth aside to tarry for a night?

Why shouldest thou be as a man astonied, as a mighty man that cannot save? yet thou, O LORD, art in the midst of us, and we are called by thy name; leave us not.

Thus saith the LORD unto this people, Thus have they loved to wander, they have not refrained their feet, therefore the LORD doth not accept them; he will now remember their iniquity, and visit their sins.

Then said the LORD ... Pray not for this people ... When they fast, I will not hear their cry; and when they offer burnt offering and an oblation, I will not accept them ... I will consume them by the sword ... by the famine ... by the pestilence.

Then said I, Ah, Lord GOD! behold, the prophets say unto them, Ye shall not see the sword, neither shall ye have famine; but I will give you assured peace in this place.

Then the LORD said unto me, The prophets prophesy lies in my name: I sent them not, neither have I commanded them, neither spake unto them: they prophesy unto you a false vision and divination, and a thing of nought, and the deceit of their heart. Therefore thus saith the LORD concerning the prophets that prophesy in my name, and I sent them not, yet they say, Sword and famine shall not be in this land; By sword and famine shall those prophets be consumed.

And the people to whom they prophesy shall be cast out in the streets of Jerusalem because of the famine and the sword; and they shall have none to bury them, them, their wives, nor their sons, nor their daughters: for I will pour their wickedness upon them.

Therefore thou shalt say this word unto them; Let mine eyes run down with tears night and day, and let them not cease: for the virgin daughter of my people is broken with a great breach, with a very grievous blow.

If I go forth into the field, then behold the slain with the sword! and if I enter into the city, then behold them that are sick with famine! yea, both the prophet and the priest go about into a land that they know not. Hast thou utterly rejected Judah? hath thy soul lothed Zion? why hast thou smitten us, and there is no healing for us? we looked for peace, and there is no good; and for the time of healing, and behold trouble! We acknowledge, O LORD, our wickedness, and the iniquity of our fathers: for we have sinned against thee. Do not abhor us, for thy name's sake, do not disgrace the throne of thy glory: remember, break not thy covenant with us.

Are there any among the vanities of the Gentiles that can cause rain? or can the heavens give showers? art not thou he, O LORD our God? therefore we will wait upon thee: for thou hast made all these things.

53. Jeremiah Prayed for Judah

Jeremiah 42:1-16 KJV

Then all the captains of the forces, and Johanan the son of Kareah, and Jezaniah the son of Hoshaiah, and all the people from the least even unto the greatest, came near, And said unto Jeremiah the prophet, Let, we beseech thee, our supplication be accepted before thee, and pray for us unto the LORD thy God, even for all this remnant; (for we are left but a few of many...) That the LORD thy God may shew us the way wherein we may walk, and the thing that we may do.

Then Jeremiah the prophet said unto them, I have heard you; behold, I will pray unto the LORD your God according to your words; and it shall come to pass, that whatsoever thing the LORD shall answer you, I will declare it unto you; I will keep nothing back from you.

Then they said to Jeremiah, The LORD be a true and faithful witness between us, if we do not even according to all things for the which the LORD thy God shall send thee to us. Whether it be good, or whether it be evil, we will obey the voice of the LORD our God, to whom we send thee; that it may be well with us, when we obey the voice of the LORD our God.

And it came to pass after ten days, that the word of the LORD came unto Jeremiah. Then called he Johanan the son of Kareah, and all the captains of the forces which were with him, and all the people from the least even to the greatest,

And said unto them, Thus saith the LORD, the God of Israel, unto whom ye sent me to present your supplication before him;

If ye will still abide in this land, then will I build you, and not pull you down, and I will plant you, and not pluck you up: for I repent me of the evil that I have done unto you. Be not afraid of the king of Babylon, of whom ye are afraid; be not afraid of him, saith the LORD: for I am with you to save you, and to deliver you from his hand.

And I will shew mercies unto you, that he may have mercy upon you, and cause you to return to your own land.

But if ye say, We will not dwell in this land, neither obey the voice of the LORD your God, Saying, No; but we will go into the land of Egypt, where we shall see no war, nor hear the sound of the trumpet, nor have hunger of bread; and there will we dwell:

And now therefore hear the word of the LORD, ye remnant of Judah; Thus saith the LORD of hosts, the God of Israel; If ye wholly set your faces to enter into Egypt, and go to sojourn there;

Then it shall come to pass, that the sword, which ye feared, shall overtake you there in the land of Egypt, and the famine, whereof ye were afraid, shall follow close after you there in Egypt; and there ye shall die.

54. Jesus Got Alone and Prayed

Luke 5:16 CEV

But Jesus would often go to some place where he could be alone and pray.

Mark 6:46 KJV

And when he had sent them away, he departed into a mountain to pray.

Matthew 14:23 KJV

And when he had sent the multitudes away, he went up into a mountain apart to pray: and when the evening was come, he was there alone.

Luke 6:12 KJV

And it came to pass in those days, that he went out into a mountain to pray, and continued all night in prayer to God.

Mark 1:35 KJV

And in the morning, rising up a great while before day, he went out, and departed into a solitary place, and there prayed.

Luke 22:39-43 CEV

Jesus went out to the Mount of Olives, as he often did, and his disciples went with him. When they got there, he told them, "Pray that you won't be tested."

Jesus walked on a little way before he knelt down and prayed, "Father, if you will, please don't make me suffer by having me drink from this cup. But do what you want, and not what I want." Then an angel from heaven came to help him. Jesus was in great pain and prayed so sincerely that his sweat fell to the ground like drops of blood.

55. Jesus' Prayer in Gethsemane

Matthew 26:36-46 KJV

Then cometh Jesus with them unto a place called Gethsemane, and saith unto the disciples, Sit ye here, while I go and pray yonder.

And he took with him Peter and the two sons of Zebedee, and began to be sorrowful and very heavy.

Then saith he unto them, My soul is exceeding sorrowful, even unto death: tarry ye here, and watch with me.

And he went a little farther, and fell on his face, and prayed, saying, O my Father, if it be possible, let this cup pass from me: nevertheless not as I will, but as thou wilt.

And he cometh unto the disciples, and findeth them asleep, and saith unto Peter, What, could ye not watch with me one hour?

Watch and pray, that ye enter not into temptation: the spirit indeed is willing, but the flesh is weak.

He went away again the second time, and prayed, saying, O my Father, if this cup may not pass away from me, except I drink it, thy will be done.

And he came and found them asleep again: for their eyes were heavy.

And he left them, and went away again, and prayed the third time, saying the same words.

Then cometh he to his disciples, and saith unto them, Sleep on now, and take your rest: behold, the hour is at hand, and the Son of man is betrayed into the hands of sinners.

Rise, let us be going: behold, he is at hand that doth me.

56. Jesus Prayed for All Believers

John 17:20-26 AMP

Neither for these alone do I pray [it is not for their sake only that I make this request], but also for all those who will ever come to believe in (trust in, cling to, rely on) Me through their word and teaching,

That they all may be one, [just] as You, Father, are in Me and I in You, that they also may be one in Us, so that the world may believe and be convinced that You have sent Me.

I have given to them the glory and honor which You have given Me, that they may be one [even] as We are one:

I in them and You in Me, in order that they may become one and perfectly united, that the world may know and [definitely] recognize that You sent Me and that You have loved them [even] as You have loved Me.

Father, I desire that they also whom You have entrusted to Me [as Your gift to Me] may be with Me where I am, so that they may see My glory, which You have given Me [Your love gift to Me]; for You loved Me before the foundation of the world.

O just and righteous Father, although the world has not known You and has failed to recognize You and has never acknowledged You, I have known You [continually]; and these men understand and know that You have sent Me.

I have made Your Name known to them and revealed Your character and Your very Self, and I will continue to make [You] known, that the love which You have bestowed upon Me may be in them [felt in their hearts] and that I [Myself] may be in them.

57. Jesus Prayed for Himself

John 17:1-5 KJV

These words spake Jesus, and lifted up his eyes to heaven, and said, Father, the hour is come; glorify thy Son, that thy Son also may glorify thee: As thou hast given him power over all flesh, that he should give eternal life to as many as thou hast given him. And this is life eternal, that they might know thee the only true God, and Jesus Christ, whom thou hast sent. I have glorified thee on the earth: I have finished the work which thou gavest me to do. And now, O Father, glorify thou me with thine own self with the glory which I had with thee before the world was.

58. Jesus Prayed for His Disciples

John 17:6-19 KJV

I have manifested thy name unto the men which thou gavest me out of the world: thine they were, and thou gavest them me; and they have kept thy word.

Now they have known that all things whatsoever thou hast given me are of thee.

For I have given unto them the words which thou gavest me; and they have received them, and have known surely that I came out from thee, and they have believed that thou didst send me.

I pray for them: I pray not for the world, but for them which thou hast given me; for they are thine.

And all mine are thine, and thine are mine; and I am glorified in them.

And now I am no more in the world, but these are in the world, and I come to thee. Holy Father, keep through thine own name those whom thou hast given me, that they may be one, as we are.

While I was with them in the world, I kept them in thy name: those that thou gavest me I have kept, and none of them is lost, but the son of perdition; that the scripture might be fulfilled.

And now come I to thee; and these things I speak in the world, that they might have my joy fulfilled in themselves.

I have given them thy word; and the world hath hated them, because they are not of the world, even as I am not of the world.

I pray not that thou shouldest take them out of the world, but that thou shouldest keep them from the evil.

They are not of the world, even as I am not of the world.

Sanctify them through thy truth: thy word is truth.

As thou hast sent me into the world, even so have I also sent them into the world.

And for their sakes I sanctify myself, that they also might be sanctified through the truth.

59. Jesus Prayed To the Father

John 12:27-29 NIV

"Now my heart is troubled, and what shall I say? 'Father, save me from this hour'? No, it was for this very reason I came to this hour. Father, glorify your name!"

Then a voice came from heaven, "I have glorified it, and will glorify it again." The crowd that was there and heard it said it had thundered; others said an angel had spoken to him.

60. Jesus' Prayer of Thanksgiving

Matthew 11:25-26 AMP

At that time Jesus began to say, I thank You, Father, Lord of heaven and earth [and I acknowledge openly and joyfully to Your honor], that You have hidden these things from the wise and clever and learned, and revealed them to babies [to the childish, untaught, and unskilled].

Yes, Father, [I praise You that] such was Your gracious will and good pleasure.

61. Jesus Prayed Then Fed the 5,000

Matthew 14:18-20 AMP

Then He ordered the crowds to recline on the grass; and He took the five loaves and the two fish, and, looking up to heaven, He gave thanks and blessed and broke the loaves and handed the pieces to the disciples, and the disciples gave them to the people.

And they all ate and were satisfied. And they picked up twelve [small hand] baskets full of the broken pieces left over.

62. Jesus Prayed At the Cross

Luke 23: 34, 46 KJV

Then said Jesus, Father, forgive them; for they know not what they do. And they parted his raiment, and cast lots.

And when Jesus had cried with a loud voice, he said, Father, into thy hands I commend my spirit: and having said thus, he gave up the ghost.

63. Jesus Prayed To Raise Lazarus

John 11:35-47 NIV

Jesus wept.

Then the Jews said, "See how he loved him!"

But some of them said, "Could not he who opened the eyes of the blind man have kept this man from dying?"

Jesus, once more deeply moved, came to the tomb. It was a cave with a stone laid across the entrance. "Take away the stone," he said.

"But, Lord," said Martha, the sister of the dead man, "by this time there is a bad odor, for he has been there four days."

Then Jesus said, "Did I not tell you that if you believed, you would see the glory of God?"

So they took away the stone. Then Jesus looked up and said, "Father, I thank you that you have heard me. I knew that you always hear me, but I said this for the benefit of the people standing here, that they may believe that you sent me."

When he had said this, Jesus called in a loud voice, "Lazarus, come out!" The dead man came out, his hands and feet wrapped with strips of linen, and a cloth around his face.

Jesus said to them, "Take off the grave clothes and let him go."

Therefore many of the Jews who had come to visit Mary, and had seen what Jesus did, put their faith in him. But some of them went to the Pharisees and told them what Jesus had done. Then the chief priests and the Pharisees called a meeting of the Sanhedrin.

64. Job Responded to the Lord

Job 42:1-12 AMP

THEN JOB said to the Lord, I know that You can do all things, and that no thought or purpose of Yours can be restrained or thwarted.

[You said to me] Who is this that darkens and obscures counsel [by words] without knowledge? Therefore [I now see] I have [rashly] uttered what I did not understand, things too wonderful for me, which I did not know.

[I had virtually said to You what You have said to me:] Hear, I beseech You, and I will speak; I will demand of You, and You declare to me. I had heard of You [only] by the hearing of the ear, but now my [spiritual] eye sees You. Therefore I loathe [my words] and abhor myself and repent in dust and ashes.

After the Lord had spoken the previous words to Job, the Lord said to Eliphaz the Temanite, My wrath is kindled against you and against your two friends, for you have not spoken of Me the thing that is right, as My servant Job has.

Now therefore take seven bullocks and seven rams and go to My servant Job and offer up for yourselves a burnt offering; and My servant Job shall pray for you, for I will accept [his prayer] that I deal not with you after your folly, in that you have not spoken of Me the thing that is right, as My servant Job has.

So Eliphaz the Temanite and Bildad the Shuhite and Zophar the Naamathite went and did as the Lord commanded them; and the Lord accepted [Job's prayer]. And the Lord turned the captivity of Job and restored his fortunes, when he prayed for his friends; also the Lord gave Job twice as much as he had before.

Then there came to him all his brothers and sisters and all who had known him before, and they ate bread with him in his house; and they sympathized with him and comforted him over all the [distressing] calamities that the Lord had brought upon him. Every man also gave him a piece of money, and every man an earring of gold.

And the Lord blessed the latter days of Job more than his beginning.

65. Jonah for Deliverance from the Whale

Jonah 1:1-7, 12, 17; 2:1-10 KJV

The word of the LORD came to Jonah son of Amittai: "Go to the great city of Nineveh and preach against it, because its wickedness has come up before me." But Jonah ran away from the LORD ... headed for Tarshish. He went down to Joppa, ... found a ship bound for that port. After paying the fare, he went aboard and sailed ...to flee from the LORD.

... the LORD sent a great wind on the sea, and such a violent storm arose that the ship threatened to break up. All the sailors were afraid and each cried out to his own god. And they threw the cargo into the sea to lighten the ship.

But Jonah had gone below deck, where he lay down and fell into a deep sleep. The captain went to him and said, "How can you sleep? Get up and call on your god! Maybe he will take notice of us, and we will not perish."

Then the sailors said to each other, "Come, let us cast lots to find out who is responsible for this calamity." They cast lots and the lot fell on Jonah. ...

"Pick me up and throw me into the sea," he replied, "and it will become calm. I know that it is my fault that this great storm has come upon you."

But the LORD provided a great fish to swallow Jonah, and Jonah was inside the fish three days and three nights.

Then Jonah prayed unto the LORD his God out of the fish's belly,

And said, I cried by reason of mine affliction unto the LORD, and he heard me; out of the belly of hell cried I, and thou heardest my voice.

For thou hadst cast me into the deep, in the midst of the seas; and the floods compassed me about: all thy billows and thy waves passed over me.

Then I said, I am cast out of thy sight; yet I will look again toward thy holy temple. The waters compassed me about, even to the soul: the depth closed me round about, the weeds were wrapped about my head.

I went down to the bottoms of the mountains; the earth with her bars was about me for ever: yet hast thou brought up my life from corruption, O LORD my God. When my soul fainted within me I remembered the LORD: and my prayer came in unto thee, into thine holy temple.

They that observe lying vanities forsake their own mercy.

But I will sacrifice unto thee with the voice of thanksgiving; I will pay that that I have vowed. Salvation is of the LORD.

And the LORD spake unto the fish, and it vomited out Jonah upon the dry land.

66. Joshua Prayed for Isreal

Joshua 7:6-15 NLT

Joshua and the elders of Israel tore their clothing in dismay, threw dust on their heads, and bowed face down to the ground before the Ark of the Lord until evening. Then Joshua cried out, "Oh, Sovereign Lord, why did you bring us across the Jordan River if you are going to let the Amorites kill us? If only we had been content to stay on the other side! Lord, what can I say now that Israel has fled from its enemies? For when the Canaanites and all the other people living in the land hear about it, they will surround us and wipe our name off the face of the earth. And then what will happen to the honor of your great name?"

But the Lord said to Joshua, "Get up! Why are you lying on your face like this? Israel has sinned and broken my covenant! They have stolen some of the things that I commanded must be set apart for me. And they have not only stolen them but have lied about it and hidden the things among their own belongings. That is why the Israelites are running from their enemies in defeat. For now Israel itself has been set apart for destruction. I will not remain with you any longer unless you destroy the things among you that were set apart for destruction.

"Get up! Command the people to purify themselves in preparation for tomorrow. For this is what the Lord, the God of Israel, says: Hidden among you, O Israel, are things set apart for the Lord. You will never defeat your enemies until you remove these things from among you.

"In the morning you must present yourselves by tribes, and the Lord will point out the tribe to which the guilty man belongs. That tribe must come forward with its clans, and the Lord will point out the guilty clan. That clan will then come forward, and the Lord will point out the guilty family. Finally, each member of the guilty family must come forward one by one. The one who has stolen what was set apart for destruction will himself be burned with fire, along with everything he has, for he has broken the covenant of the Lord and has done a horrible thing in Israel."

67. King Asa Prayed for God's Victory

2 Chronicle 14:2-13 NIV

Asa did what was good and right in the eyes of the LORD his God. He removed the foreign altars and the high places, smashed the sacred stones and cut down the Asherah poles. He commanded Judah to seek the LORD, the God of their fathers, and to obey his laws and commands. He removed the high places and incense altars in every town in Judah, and the kingdom was at peace under him. He built up the fortified cities of Judah, since the land was at peace. No one was at war with him during those years, for the LORD gave him rest.

"Let us build up these towns," he said to Judah, "and put walls around them, with towers, gates and bars. The land is still ours, because we have sought the LORD our God; we sought him and he has given us rest on every side." So they built and prospered.

Asa had an army of three hundred thousand men from Judah, equipped with large shields and with spears, and two hundred and eighty thousand from Benjamin, armed with small shields and with bows. All these were brave fighting men.

Zerah the Cushite marched out against them with a vast army and three hundred chariots, and came as far as Mareshah. Asa went out to meet him, and they took up battle positions in the Valley of Zephathah near Mareshah.

Then Asa called to the LORD his God and said, "LORD, there is no one like you to help the powerless against the mighty. Help us, O LORD our God, for we rely on you, and in your name we have come against this vast army. O LORD, you are our God; do not let man prevail against you."

The LORD struck down the Cushites before Asa and Judah. The Cushites fled, and Asa and his army pursued them as far as

Gerar. Such a great number of Cushites fell that they could not recover; they were crushed before the LORD and his forces. The men of Judah carried off a large amount of plunder. They destroyed all the villages around Gerar, for the terror of the LORD had fallen upon them. They plundered all these villages, since there was much booty there. They also attacked the camps of the herdsmen and carried off droves of sheep and goats and camels. Then they returned to Jerusalem.

68. Manasseh Sought the Lord

2 Chronicles 33:1-20 KJV

Manasseh was twelve years old when he began to reign, and he reigned fifty and five years in Jerusalem: But did that which was evil in the sight of the LORD, like unto the abominations of the heathen, whom the LORD had cast out before the children of Israel. For he built again the high places which Hezekiah his father had broken down, and he reared up altars for Baalim, and made groves, and worshipped all the host of heaven, and served them.

Also he built altars in the house of the LORD ... caused his children to pass through the fire in the valley of the son of Hinnom: also he observed times, and used enchantments, and used witchcraft, and dealt with a familiar spirit, and with wizards: he wrought much evil in the sight of the LORD, to provoke him to anger.

And he set a carved image, the idol which he had made, in the house of God, of which God had said to David and to Solomon his son, In this house, and in Jerusalem, which I have chosen before all the tribes of Israel, will I put my name for ever ...

And the LORD spake to Manasseh, and to his people: but they would not hearken.

Wherefore the LORD brought upon them the captains of the host of the king of Assyria, which took Manasseh among the thorns, and bound him with fetters, and carried him to Babylon.

And when he was in affliction, he besought the LORD his God, and humbled himself greatly before the God of his fathers,

And prayed unto him: and he was intreated of him, and heard his supplication, and brought him again to Jerusalem into his kingdom. Then Manasseh knew that the LORD he was God.

Now after this he built a wall without the city of David, on the west side of Gihon, in the valley, even to the entering in at the fish gate, and compassed about Ophel, and raised it up a very great height, and put captains of war in all the fenced cities of Judah. And he took away the strange gods, and the idol out of the house of the LORD, and all the altars that he had built in the mount of the house of the LORD ... And he repaired the altar of the LORD, and sacrificed thereon peace offerings and thank offerings, and commanded Judah to serve the LORD God of Israel.

Nevertheless the people did sacrifice still in the high places, yet unto the LORD their God only. Now the rest of the acts of Manasseh, and his prayer unto his God, and the words of the seers that spake to him in the name of the LORD God of Israel ... His prayer also, and how God was intreated of him, and all his sins, and his trespass, and the places wherein he built high places, and set up groves and graven images, before he was humbled: behold, they are written among the sayings of the seers.

So Manasseh slept with his fathers, and they buried him in his own house: and Amon his son reigned in his stead.

69. Manoah for Guidance for Unborn Child

Judges 13:8-21, 24 KJV

Then Manoah intreated the LORD, and said, O my Lord, let the man of God which thou didst send come again unto us, and teach us what we shall do unto the child that shall be born.

And God hearkened to the voice of Manoah; and the angel of God came again unto the woman as she sat in the field: but Manoah her husband was not with her. And the woman made haste, and ran, and shewed her husband, and said unto him, Behold, the man hath appeared unto me, that came unto me the other day.

And Manoah arose, and went after his wife, and came to the man, and said unto him, Art thou the man that spakest unto the woman? And he said, I am. And Manoah said, Now let thy words come to pass. How shall we order the child, and how shall we do unto him?

And the angel of the LORD said unto Manoah, Of all that I said unto the woman let her beware. She may not eat of any thing that cometh of the vine, neither let her drink wine or strong drink, nor eat any unclean thing: all that I commanded her let her observe.

And Manoah said unto the angel of the LORD, I pray thee, let us detain thee, until we shall have made ready a kid for thee.

And the angel of the LORD said unto Manoah, Though thou detain me, I will not eat of thy bread: and if thou wilt offer a burnt offering, thou must offer it unto the LORD. For Manoah knew not that he was an angel of the LORD.

And Manoah said unto the angel of the LORD, What is thy name, that when thy sayings come to pass we may do thee honour?

And the angel of the LORD said unto him, Why askest thou thus after my name, seeing it is secret?

So Manoah took a kid with a meat offering, and offered it upon a rock unto the LORD: and the angel did wonderously; and Manoah and his wife looked on. For it came to pass, when the flame went up toward heaven from off the altar, that the angel of the LORD ascended in the flame of the altar. And Manoah and his wife looked on it, and fell on their faces to the ground.

But the angel of the LORD did no more appear to Manoah and to his wife. Then Manoah knew that he was an angel of the LORD ...

And the woman bare a son, and called his name Samson: and the child grew, and the LORD blessed him.

70. Melchizedek Victory Offering for Abraham

Genesis 14:17-20 CEV

Abram returned after he had defeated King Chedorlaomer and the other kings. Then the king of Sodom went to meet Abram in Shaveh Valley, which is also known as King's Valley.

King Melchizedek of Salem was a priest of God Most High. He brought out some bread and wine and said to Abram:

"I bless you in the name of God Most High, Creator of heaven and earth.

All praise belongs to God Most High for helping you defeat your enemies."

Then Abram gave Melchizedek a tenth of everything.

Hebrews 7:1-4 CEV

Melchizedek was both king of Salem and priest of God Most High. He was the one who went out and gave Abraham his blessing, when Abraham returned from killing the kings. Then Abraham gave him a tenth of everything he had.

The meaning of the name Melchizedek is "King of Justice." But since Salem means "peace," he is also "King of Peace." We are not told that he had a father or mother or ancestors or beginning or end. He is like the Son of God and will be a priest forever. Notice how great Melchizedek is! Our famous ancestor Abraham gave him a tenth of what he had taken from his enemies.

71. Moses Prayed for Pharaoh

Exodus 8:8-15, 30-32, 9:33-35, 10:18-20 NIV

Pharaoh summoned Moses and Aaron and said, "Pray to the LORD to take the frogs away from me and my people, and I will let your people go to offer sacrifices to the LORD."

Moses said to Pharaoh, "I leave to you the honor of setting the time for me to pray for you and your officials and your people that you and your houses may be rid of the frogs, except for those that remain in the Nile."

"Tomorrow," Pharaoh said.

Moses replied, "It will be as you say, so that you may know there is no one like the LORD our God. The frogs will leave you and your houses, your officials and your people; they will remain only in the Nile."

After Moses and Aaron left Pharaoh, Moses cried out to the LORD about the frogs he had brought on Pharaoh. And the LORD did what Moses asked. The frogs died in the houses, in the courtyards and in the fields. They were piled into heaps, and the land reeked of them. But when Pharaoh saw that there was relief, he hardened his heart and would not listen to Moses and Aaron, just as the LORD had said ...

Then Moses left Pharaoh and prayed to the LORD, and the LORD did what Moses asked: The flies left Pharaoh and his officials and his people; not a fly remained. But this time also Pharaoh hardened his heart and would not let the people go ...

Then Moses left Pharaoh and went out of the city. He spread out his hands toward the LORD; the thunder and hail stopped, and the rain no longer poured down on the land. When Pharaoh saw that the rain and hail and thunder had stopped, he sinned again: He and his officials hardened their hearts. So Pharaoh's heart was hard and he would not let the Israelites go, just as the LORD had said through Moses ...

Moses then left Pharaoh and prayed to the LORD. And the LORD changed the wind to a very strong west wind, which caught up the locusts and carried them into the Red Sea. Not a locust was left anywhere in Egypt. But the LORD hardened Pharaoh's heart, and he would not let the Israelites go ...

72. Moses - Face to Face with God

Exodus 33:7-23 NIV

Now Moses used to take a tent and pitch it outside the camp some distance away, calling it the "tent of meeting." Anyone inquiring of the LORD would go to the tent of meeting outside the camp. And whenever Moses went out to the tent, all the people rose and stood at the entrances to their tents, watching Moses until he entered the tent. As Moses went into the tent, the pillar of cloud would come down and stay at the entrance, while the LORD spoke with Moses. Whenever the people saw the pillar of cloud standing at the entrance to the tent, they all stood and worshiped, each at the entrance to his tent. The LORD would speak to Moses face to face, as a man speaks with his friend. Then Moses would return to the camp, but his young aide Joshua son of Nun did not leave the tent.

Moses said to the LORD, "You have been telling me, 'Lead these people,' but you have not let me know whom you will send with me. You have said, 'I know you by name and you have found favor with me.' If you are pleased with me, teach me your ways so I may know you and continue to find favor with you. Remember that this nation is your people."

The LORD replied, "My Presence will go with you, and I will give you rest."

Then Moses said to him, "If your Presence does not go with us, do not send us up from here. How will anyone know that you are pleased with me and with your people unless you go with us? What else will distinguish me and your people from all the other people on the face of the earth?"

And the LORD said to Moses, "I will do the very thing you have asked, because I am pleased with you and I know you by name."

Then Moses said, "Now show me your glory."

And the LORD said, "I will cause all my goodness to pass in front of you, and I will proclaim my name, the LORD, in your presence. I will have mercy on whom I will have mercy, and I will have compassion on whom I will have compassion. But," he said, "you cannot see my face, for no one may see me and live."

Then the LORD said, "There is a place near me where you may stand on a rock. When my glory passes by, I will put you in a cleft in the rock and cover you with my hand until I have passed by. Then I will remove my hand and you will see my back; but my face must not be seen."

73. Moses Prayed for Mariam

Number 12:9-15 KJV

The anger of the LORD burned against them, and he left them.

When the cloud lifted from above the Tent, there stood Miriam—leprous, like snow. Aaron turned toward her and saw that she had leprosy; and he said to Moses, "Please, my lord, do not hold against us the sin we have so foolishly committed. Do not let her be like a stillborn infant coming from its mother's womb with its flesh half eaten away."

So Moses cried out to the LORD, "O God, please heal her!"

The LORD replied to Moses, "If her father had spit in her face, would she not have been in disgrace for seven days? Confine her outside the camp for seven days; after that she can be brought back." So Miriam was confined outside the camp for seven days, and the people did not move on till she was brought back.

74. Moses Prayed for Water in Marah

Exodus 15:23-25 KJV

And when they came to Marah, they could not drink of the waters of Marah, for they were bitter: therefore the name of it was called Marah. And the people murmured against Moses, saying, What shall we drink?

And he cried unto the LORD; and the LORD shewed him a tree, which when he had cast into the waters, the waters were made sweet: there he made for them a statute and an ordinance, and there he proved them.

75. Moses Prayed for Water at Mount Sinai

Exodus 17:3-6 CEV

But the people were thirsty and kept on complaining, " Moses, did you bring us out of Egypt just to let us and our families and our animals die of thirst?" Then Moses prayed to the LORD, " What am I going to do with these people? They are about to stone me to death!"

The LORD answered, " Take some of the leaders with you and go ahead of the rest of the people. Also take along the walking stick you used to strike the Nile River, and when you get to the rock at Mount Sinai, I will be there with you. Strike the rock with the stick, and water will pour out for the people to drink." Moses did this while the leaders watched.

76. Moses Prayed for Water at Kadesh

Numbers 20:3-12 KJV

And the people chode with Moses, and spake, saying, Would God that we had died when our brethren died before the LORD! And why have ye brought up the congregation of the LORD into this wilderness, that we and our cattle should die ...

And wherefore have ye made us to come up out of Egypt, to bring us in unto this evil place? it is no place of seed, or of figs, or of vines, or of pomegranates; neither is there any water to drink.

And Moses and Aaron went from the presence of the assembly unto the door of the tabernacle of the congregation, and they fell upon their faces: and the glory of the LORD appeared unto them.

And the LORD spake unto Moses, saying, Take the rod, and gather thou the assembly together, thou, and Aaron thy brother, and speak ye unto the rock before their eyes; and it shall give forth his water, and thou shalt bring forth to them water out of the rock: so thou shalt give the congregation and their beasts drink.

And Moses took the rod from before the LORD, as he commanded him. And Moses and Aaron gathered the congregation together before the rock, and he said unto them, Hear now, ye rebels; must we fetch you water out of this rock?

And Moses lifted up his hand, and with his rod he smote the rock twice: and the water came out abundantly, and the congregation drank, and their beasts also.

And the LORD spake unto Moses and Aaron, Because ye believed me not, to sanctify me in the eyes of the children of Israel, therefore ye shall not bring this congregation into the land which I have given them.

77. Moses Prayed for Israel's Forgiveness

Deuteronomy 9:16-29 KJV

And I looked, and, behold, ye had sinned against the LORD your God, and had made you a molten calf: ye had turned aside quickly out of the way which the LORD had commanded you.

And I took the two tables, and cast them out of my two hands, and brake them before your eyes.

And I fell down before the LORD, as at the first, forty days and forty nights: I did neither eat bread, nor drink water, because of all your sins which ye sinned, in doing wickedly in the sight of the LORD, to provoke him to anger. For I was afraid of the anger and hot displeasure, wherewith the LORD was wroth against you to destroy you. But the LORD hearkened unto me at that time also.

And the LORD was very angry with Aaron to have destroyed him: and I prayed for Aaron also the same time.

And I took your sin, the calf which ye had made, and burnt it with fire, and stamped it, and ground it very small, even until it was as small as dust: and I cast the dust thereof into the brook that descended out of the mount.

And at Taberah, and at Massah, and at Kibrothhattaavah, ye provoked the LORD to wrath. Likewise when the LORD sent you from Kadeshbarnea, saying, Go up and possess the land which I have given you; then ye rebelled against the commandment of the LORD your God, and ye believed him not, nor hearkened to his voice.

Ye have been rebellious against the LORD from the day that I knew you.

Thus I fell down before the LORD forty days and forty nights, as I fell down at the first; because the LORD had said he would destroy you.

I prayed therefore unto the LORD, and said, O Lord GOD, destroy not thy people and thine inheritance, which thou hast redeemed through thy greatness, which thou hast brought forth out of Egypt with a mighty hand.

Remember thy servants, Abraham, Isaac, and Jacob; look not unto the stubbornness of this people, nor to their wickedness, nor to their sin:

Lest the land whence thou broughtest us out say, Because the LORD was not able to bring them into the land which he promised them, and because he hated them, he hath brought them out to slay them in the wilderness.

Yet they are thy people and thine inheritance, which thou broughtest out by thy mighty power and by thy stretched out arm.

78. Naomi Prayed for Ruth and Oprah

Ruth 1:1-14 CEV

Before Israel was ruled by kings, Elimelech from the tribe of Ephrath lived in the town of Bethlehem. His wife was named Naomi, and their two sons were Mahlon and Chilion. But when their crops failed, they moved to the country of Moab. And while they were there, Elimelech died, leaving Naomi with only her two sons. Later, Naomi's sons married Moabite women. One was named Orpah and the other Ruth. About ten years later, Mahlon and Chilion also died. Now Naomi had no husband or sons.

When Naomi heard that the LORD had given his people a good harvest, she and her two daughters-in-law got ready to leave Moab and go to Judah. As they were on their way there, Naomi said to them, "Don't you want to go back home to your own mothers? You were kind to my husband and sons, and you have always been kind to me.

I pray that the LORD will be just as kind to you. May he give each of you another husband and a home of your own."

Naomi kissed them. They cried and said, "We want to go with you and live among your people."

But she replied, "My daughters, why don't you return home? What good will it do you to go with me? Do you think I could have more sons for you to marry? You must go back home, because I am too old to marry again. Even if I got married tonight and later had more sons, would you wait for them to become old enough to marry? No, my daughters! Life is harder for me than it is for you, because the LORD has turned against me." They cried again. Orpah kissed her mother-in-law good-by, but Ruth held on to her.

79. Nehemiah Prepared to Build the Wall

Nehemiah 1:1-11 AMP

The Words or story of Nehemiah son of Hacaliah: Now in the month of Chislev in the twentieth year [of the Persian king], as I was in the castle of Shushan,

Hanani, one of my kinsmen, came with certain men from Judah, and I asked them about the surviving Jews who had escaped exile, and about Jerusalem.

And they said to me, The remnant there in the province who escaped exile are in great trouble and reproach; the wall of Jerusalem is broken down, and its [fortified] gates are destroyed by fire.

When I heard this, I sat down and wept and mourned for days and fasted and prayed [constantly] before the God of heaven,

And I said, O Lord God of heaven, the great and terrible God, Who keeps covenant, loving-kindness, and mercy for those who love Him and keep His commandments,

Let Your ear now be attentive and Your eyes open to listen to the prayer of Your servant which I pray before You day and night for the Israelites, Your servants, confessing the sins of the Israelites which we have sinned against You. Yes, I and my father's house have sinned.

We have acted very corruptly against You and have not kept the commandments, statutes, and ordinances which You commanded Your servant Moses.

Remember [earnestly] what You commanded Your servant Moses: If you transgress and are unfaithful, I will scatter you abroad among the nations;

But if you return to Me and keep My commandments and do them, though your outcasts were in the farthest part of the heavens [the expanse of outer space], yet will I gather them from there and will bring them to the place in which I have chosen to set My Name.

Now these are Your servants and Your people, whom You have redeemed by Your great power and by Your strong hand.

O Lord, let Your ear be attentive to the prayer of Your servant and the prayer of Your servants who delight to revere and fear Your name (Your nature and attributes); and prosper, I pray You, Your servant this day and grant him mercy in the sight of this man. For I was cupbearer to the king.

80. Nehemiah Lead Israel in Confessing Their Sins

Nehemiah 9:1-8 KJV

Now in the twenty and fourth day of this month the children of Israel were assembled with fasting, and with sackclothes, and earth upon them.

And the seed of Israel separated themselves from all strangers, and stood and confessed their sins, and the iniquities of their fathers.

And they stood up in their place, and read in the book of the law of the LORD their God one fourth part of the day; and another fourth part they confessed, and worshipped the LORD their God.

Then stood up upon the stairs, of the Levites, Jeshua, and Bani, Kadmiel, Shebaniah, Bunni, Sherebiah, Bani, and Chenani, and cried with a loud voice unto the LORD their God.

Then the Levites, Jeshua, and Kadmiel, Bani, Hashabniah, Sherebiah, Hodijah, Shebaniah, and Pethahiah, said, Stand up and bless the LORD your God for ever and ever: and blessed be thy glorious name, which is exalted above all blessing and praise.

Thou, even thou, art LORD alone; thou hast made heaven, the heaven of heavens, with all their host, the earth, and all things that are therein, the seas, and all that is therein, and thou preservest them all; and the host of heaven worshippeth thee.

Thou art the LORD the God, who didst choose Abram, and broughtest him forth out of Ur of the Chaldees, and gavest him the name of Abraham;

And foundest his heart faithful before thee, and madest a covenant with him to give the land of the Canaanites, the Hittites, the Amorites, and the Perizzites, and the Jebusites, and the Girgashites, to give it, I say, to his seed, and hast performed thy words; for thou art righteous:

81. Paul and Ananias

Acts 9:3-20 KJV

And as he journeyed, he came near Damascus: and suddenly there shined round about him a light from heaven: And he fell to the earth, and heard a voice saying unto him, Saul, Saul, why persecutest thou me?

And he said, Who art thou, Lord? And the Lord said, I am Jesus whom thou persecutest: it is hard for thee to kick against the pricks.

And he trembling and astonished said, Lord, what wilt thou have me to do? And the Lord said unto him, Arise, and go into the city, and it shall be told thee what thou must do. And the men which journeyed with him stood speechless, hearing a voice, but seeing no man.

And Saul arose from the earth; and when his eyes were opened, he saw no man: but they led him by the hand, and brought him into Damascus.

And he was three days without sight, and neither did eat nor drink.

And there was a certain disciple at Damascus, named Ananias; and to him said the Lord in a vision, Ananias. And he said, Behold, I am here, Lord.

And the Lord said unto him, Arise, and go into the street which is called Straight, and enquire in the house of Judas for one called Saul, of Tarsus: for, behold, he prayeth, And hath seen in a vision a man named Ananias coming in, and putting his hand on him, that he might receive his sight.

Then Ananias answered, Lord, I have heard by many of this man, how much evil he hath done to thy saints at Jerusalem:

And here he hath authority from the chief priests to bind all that call on thy name. But the Lord said unto him, Go thy way: for he is a chosen vessel unto me, to bear my name before the Gentiles, and kings, and the children of Israel:

For I will shew him how great things he must suffer for my name's sake.

And Ananias went his way, and entered into the house; and putting his hands on him said, Brother Saul, the Lord, even Jesus, that appeared unto thee in the way as thou camest, hath sent me, that thou mightest receive thy sight, and be filled with the Holy Ghost.

And immediately there fell from his eyes as it had been scales: and he received sight forthwith, and arose, and was baptized.

And when he had received meat, he was strengthened. Then was Saul certain days with the disciples which were at Damascus.

And straightway he preached Christ in the synagogues, that he is the Son of God.

82. Paul and Silas Prayed & Sang in Prison

Acts 16:23-36 KJV

And when they had laid many stripes upon them, they cast them into prison, charging the jailor to keep them safely:

Who, having received such a charge, thrust them into the inner prison, and made their feet fast in the stocks.

And at midnight Paul and Silas prayed, and sang praises unto God: and the prisoners heard them.

And suddenly there was a great earthquake, so that the foundations of the prison were shaken: and immediately all the doors were opened, and every one's bands were loosed.

And the keeper of the prison awaking out of his sleep, and seeing the prison doors open, he drew out his sword, and would have killed himself, supposing that the prisoners had been fled.

But Paul cried with a loud voice, saying, Do thyself no harm: for we are all here.

Then he called for a light, and sprang in, and came trembling, and fell down before Paul and Silas,

And brought them out, and said, Sirs, what must I do to be saved?

And they said, Believe on the Lord Jesus Christ, and thou shalt be saved, and thy house.

And they spake unto him the word of the Lord, and to all that were in his house.

And he took them the same hour of the night, and washed their stripes; and was baptized, he and all his, straightway.

And when he had brought them into his house, he set meat before them, and rejoiced, believing in God with all his house.

And when it was day, the magistrates sent the serjeants, saying, Let those men go.

And the keeper of the prison told this saying to Paul, The magistrates have sent to let you go: now therefore depart, and go in peace.

83. Paul Prayed for Elders

Acts 14:23 KJV

And when they had ordained them elders in every church, and had prayed with fasting, they commended them to the Lord, on whom they believed.

84. Paul Prayed for Agrippa

Acts 20:36-38 KJV

And when he had thus spoken, he kneeled down, and prayed with them all. And they all wept sore, and fell on Paul's neck, and kissed him, Sorrowing most of all for the words which he spake, that they should see his face no more. And they accompanied him unto the ship.

85. Paul Prayed for Agrippa

Acts 26:25-29 NIV

"I am not insane, most excellent Festus," Paul replied. "What I am saying is true and reasonable. The king is familiar with these things, and I can speak freely to him. I am convinced that none of this has escaped his notice, because it was not done in a corner. King Agrippa, do you believe the prophets? I know you do."

Then Agrippa said to Paul, "Do you think that in such a short time you can persuade me to be a Christian?"

Paul replied, "Short time or long—I pray God that not only you but all who are listening to me today may become what I am, except for these chains."

86. Paul Prayed for the Father of Publius

Acts 28:7-9 KJV

In the same quarters were possessions of the chief man of the island, whose name was Publius; who received us, and lodged us three days courteously. And it came to pass, that the father of Publius lay sick of a fever and of a bloody flux: to whom Paul entered in, and prayed, and laid his hands on him, and healed him. So when this was done, others also, which had diseases in the island, came, and were healed:

87. Paul Prayed for the Thessalonians

1 Thessalonians 1:1-3 NIV

Paul, Silas and Timothy, To the church of the Thessalonians in God the Father and the Lord Jesus Christ: Grace and peace to you.

Thanksgiving for the Thessalonians' Faith We always thank God for all of you, mentioning you in our prayers. We continually remember before our God and Father your work produced by faith, your labor prompted by love, and your endurance inspired by hope in our Lord Jesus Christ.

88. Paul Prayed for the Church at Philemon

Philemon 1:-5 NLT

I am writing to Philemon, our beloved co-worker, and to our sister Apphia, and to our fellow soldier Archippus, and to the church that meets in your house. May God our Father and the Lord Jesus Christ give you grace and peace. I always thank my God when I pray for you.

89. Paul Prayed for the Ephesians

Ephesians 1:15-23 KJV

Wherefore I also, after I heard of your faith in the Lord Jesus, and love unto all the saints,

Cease not to give thanks for you, making mention of you in my prayers;

That the God of our Lord Jesus Christ, the Father of glory, may give unto you the spirit of wisdom and revelation in the knowledge of him:

The eyes of your understanding being enlightened; that ye may know what is the hope of his calling, and what the riches of the glory of his inheritance in the saints,

And what is the exceeding greatness of his power to us-ward who believe, according to the working of his mighty power,

Which he wrought in Christ, when he raised him from the dead, and set him at his own right hand in the heavenly places,

Far above all principality, and power, and might, and dominion, and every name that is named, not only in this world, but also in that which is to come:

And hath put all things under his feet, and gave him to be the head over all things to the church,

Which is his body, the fulness of him that filleth all in all.

90. Paul Prayer for Believers

Ephesians 3:12-21 NIV

In him and through faith in him we may approach God with freedom and confidence. I ask you, therefore, not to be discouraged because of my sufferings for you, which are your glory.

For this reason I kneel before the Father, from whom his whole family in heaven and on earth derives its name. I pray that out of his glorious riches he may strengthen you with power through his Spirit in your inner being, so that Christ may dwell in your hearts through faith. And I pray that you, being rooted and established in love, may have power, together with all the saints, to grasp how wide and long and high and deep is the love of Christ, and to know this love that surpasses knowledge—that you may be filled to the measure of all the fullness of God.

Now to him who is able to do immeasurably more than all we ask or imagine, according to his power that is at work within us, to him be glory in the church and in Christ Jesus throughout all generations, for ever and ever! Amen.

91. Paul Prayed for the Philippians

Philippians 1:9-11 AMP

And this I pray: that your love may abound yet more and more and extend to its fullest development in knowledge and all keen insight [that your love may display itself in greater depth of acquaintance and more comprehensive discernment],

So that you may surely learn to sense what is vital, and approve and prize what is excellent and of real value [recognizing the highest and the best, and distinguishing the moral differences], and that you may be untainted and pure and unerring and blameless [so that with hearts sincere and certain and unsullied, you may approach] the day of Christ [not stumbling nor causing others to stumble].

May you abound in and be filled with the fruits of righteousness (of right standing with God and right doing) which come through Jesus Christ (the Anointed One), to the honor and praise of God [that His glory may be both manifested and recognized].

92. Paul Prayed for the Corinthians

2 Corinthians 13:7 KJV

Now I pray to God that ye do no evil; not that we should appear approved, but that ye should do that which is honest, though we be as reprobates.

93. Paul Prayed For the Colossians

Colossians 1:1-18 KJV

Paul, an apostle of Jesus Christ by the will of God, and Timotheus our brother,

To the saints and faithful brethren in Christ which are at Colosse: Grace be unto you, and peace, from God our Father and the Lord Jesus Christ.

We give thanks to God and the Father of our Lord Jesus Christ, praying always for you, Since we heard of your faith in Christ Jesus, and of the love which ye have to all the saints,

For the hope which is laid up for you in heaven, whereof ye heard before in the word of the truth of the gospel; Which is come unto you, as it is in all the world; and bringeth forth fruit, as it doth also in you, since the day ye heard of it, and knew the grace of God in truth:

As ye also learned of Epaphras our dear fellowservant, who is for you a faithful minister of Christ;

Who also declared unto us your love in the Spirit.

For this cause we also, since the day we heard it, do not cease to pray for you, and to desire that ye might be filled with the knowledge of his will in all wisdom and spiritual understanding;

That ye might walk worthy of the Lord unto all pleasing, being fruitful in every good work, and increasing in the knowledge of God;

Strengthened with all might, according to his glorious power, unto all patience and longsuffering with joyfulness; Giving thanks unto the Father, which hath made us meet to be partakers of the inheritance of the saints in light: Who hath delivered us from the power of darkness, and hath translated us into the kingdom of his dear Son: In whom we have redemption through his blood, even the forgiveness of sins:

Who is the image of the invisible God, the firstborn of every creature:

For by him were all things created, that are in heaven, and that are in earth, visible and invisible, whether they be thrones, or dominions, or principalities, or powers: all things were created by him, and for him:

And he is before all things, and by him all things consist.

And he is the head of the body, the church: who is the beginning, the firstborn from the dead; that in all things he might have the preeminence.

94. Paul Requested Prayer

Romans 15:30-32 KJV

Now I beseech you, brethren, for the Lord Jesus Christ's sake, and for the love of the Spirit, that ye strive together with me in your prayers to God for me;

That I may be delivered from them that do not believe in Judaea; and that my service which I have for Jerusalem may be accepted of the saints;

That I may come unto you with joy by the will of God, and may with you be refreshed.

2 Thessalonians 3:1-5 NLT

Finally, dear brothers and sisters, we ask you to pray for us. Pray that the Lord's message will spread rapidly and be honored wherever it goes, just as when it came to you.

Pray, too, that we will be rescued from wicked and evil people, for not everyone is a believer. But the Lord is faithful; he will strengthen you and guard you from the evil one.

And we are confident in the Lord that you are doing and will continue to do the things we commanded you. May the Lord lead your hearts into a full understanding and expression of the love of God and the patient endurance that comes from Christ.

95. Peter Prayed to Raise Dorcas from the Dead

Acts 9:36-43 AMP

Now there was at Joppa a disciple [a woman] named [in Aramaic] Tabitha, which [in Greek] means Dorcas. She was abounding in good deeds and acts of charity.

About that time she fell sick and died, and when they had cleansed her, they laid [her] in an upper room.

Since Lydda was near Joppa [however], the disciples, hearing that Peter was there, sent two men to him begging him, Do come to us without delay.

So Peter [immediately] rose and accompanied them. And when he had arrived, they took him to the upper room. All the widows stood around him, crying and displaying undershirts (tunics) and [other] garments such as Dorcas was accustomed to make while she was with them.

But Peter put them all out [of the room] and knelt down and prayed; then turning to the body he said, Tabitha, get up! And she opened her eyes; and when she saw Peter, she raised herself and sat upright.

And he gave her his hand and lifted her up. Then calling in God's people and the widows, he presented her to them alive.

And this became known throughout all Joppa, and many came to believe on the Lord [to adhere to and trust in and rely on Him as the Christ and as their Savior].

And Peter remained in Joppa for considerable time with a certain Simon a tanner.

96. Samson Prayed for Strength One Last Time

Judges 16:18-31 NIV

When Delilah saw that he had told her everything, she sent word to the rulers of the Philistines, "Come back once more; he has told me everything." So the rulers of the Philistines returned with the silver in their hands. Having put him to sleep on her lap, she called a man to shave off the seven braids of his hair, and so began to subdue him. And his strength left him.

Then she called, "Samson, the Philistines are upon you!"

He awoke from his sleep and thought, "I'll go out as before and shake myself free." But he did not know that the LORD had left him.

Then the Philistines seized him, gouged out his eyes and took him down to Gaza. Binding him with bronze shackles, they set him to grinding in the prison. But the hair on his head began to grow again after it had been shaved.

Now the rulers of the Philistines assembled to offer a great sacrifice to Dagon their god and to celebrate, saying, "Our god has delivered Samson, our enemy, into our hands." When the people saw him, they praised their god, saying, "Our god has delivered our enemy into our hands, the one who laid waste our land and multiplied our slain."

While they were in high spirits, they shouted, "Bring out Samson to entertain us." So they called Samson out of the prison, and he performed for them. When they stood him among the pillars, Samson said to the servant who held his hand, "Put me where I can feel the pillars that support the temple, so that I may lean against them." Now the temple was crowded with men and women; all the rulers of the Philistines were there, and on the roof were about three thousand men and women watching Samson perform. Then Samson prayed to the LORD, "O Sovereign LORD, remember me. O God, please strengthen me just once more, and let me with one blow get revenge on the Philistines for my two eyes." Then Samson reached toward the two central pillars on which the temple stood. Bracing himself against them, his right hand on the one and his left hand on the other, Samson said, "Let me die with the Philistines!" Then he pushed with all his might, and down came the temple on the rulers and all the people in it. Thus he killed many more when he died than while he lived.

Then his brothers and his father's whole family went down to get him. They brought him back and buried him between Zorah and Eshtaol in the tomb of Manoah his father. He had led Israel twenty years.

97. Samuel Prayed for Israel

1 Samuel 7:3-15 KJV

And Samuel spake unto all the house of Israel, saying, If ye do return unto the LORD with all your hearts, then put away the strange gods and Ashtaroth from among you, and prepare your hearts unto the LORD, and serve him only: and he will deliver you out of the hand of the Philistines.

Then the children of Israel did put away Baalim and Ashtaroth, and served the LORD only. And Samuel said, Gather all Israel to Mizpeh, and I will pray for you unto the LORD.

And they gathered together to Mizpeh, and drew water, and poured it out before the LORD, and fasted on that day, and said there, We have sinned against the LORD. And Samuel judged the children of Israel in Mizpeh.

And when the Philistines heard that the children of Israel were gathered together to Mizpeh, the lords of the Philistines went up against Israel. And when the children of Israel heard it, they were afraid of the Philistines.

And the children of Israel said to Samuel, Cease not to cry unto the LORD our God for us, that he will save us out of the hand of the Philistines.

And Samuel took a sucking lamb, and offered it for a burnt offering wholly unto the LORD: and Samuel cried unto the LORD for Israel; and the LORD heard him.

And as Samuel was offering up the burnt offering, the Philistines drew near to battle against Israel: but the LORD thundered with a great thunder on that day upon the Philistines, and discomfited them; and they were smitten before Israel. And the men of Israel went out of Mizpeh, and pursued the Philistines, and smote them, until they came under Bethcar.

Then Samuel took a stone, and set it between Mizpeh and Shen, and called the name of it Ebenezer, saying, Hitherto hath the LORD helped us.

So the Philistines were subdued, and they came no more into the coast of Israel: and the hand of the LORD was against the Philistines all the days of Samuel.

And the cities which the Philistines had taken from Israel were restored to Israel, from Ekron even unto Gath; and the coasts thereof did Israel deliver out of the hands of the Philistines. And there was peace between Israel and the Amorites.

And Samuel judged Israel all the days of his life.

98. Solomon Asked for Wisdom

1 King 3:1-15 KJV

And Solomon made affinity with Pharaoh king of Egypt, and took Pharaoh's daughter, and brought her into the city of David, until he had made an end of building his own house, and the house of the LORD, and the wall of Jerusalem round about. Only the people sacrificed in high places, because there was no house built unto the name of the LORD, until those days.

And Solomon loved the LORD, walking in the statutes of David his father: only he sacrificed and burnt incense in high places.

And the king went to Gibeon to sacrifice there; for that was the great high place: a thousand burnt offerings did Solomon offer upon that altar.

In Gibeon the LORD appeared to Solomon in a dream by night: and God said, Ask what I shall give thee.

And Solomon said, Thou hast shewed unto thy servant David my father great mercy, according as he walked before thee in truth, and in righteousness, and in uprightness of heart with thee; and thou hast kept for him this great kindness, that thou hast given him a son to sit on his throne, as it is this day.

And now, O LORD my God, thou hast made thy servant king instead of David my father: and I am but a little child: I know not how to go out or come in. And thy servant is in the midst of thy people which thou hast chosen, a great people, that cannot be numbered nor counted for multitude.

Give therefore thy servant an understanding heart to judge thy people, that I may discern between good and bad: for who is able to judge this thy so great a people? And the speech pleased the LORD, that Solomon had asked this thing.

And God said unto him, Because thou hast asked this thing, and hast not asked for thyself long life; neither hast asked riches for thyself, nor hast asked the life of thine enemies; but hast asked for thyself understanding to discern judgment; Behold, I have done according to thy words: lo, I have given thee a wise and an understanding heart; so that there was none like thee before thee, neither after thee shall any arise like unto thee.

And I have also given thee that which thou hast not asked, both riches, and honour: so that there shall not be any among the kings like unto thee all thy days.

And if thou wilt walk in my ways, to keep my statutes and my commandments, as thy father David did walk, then I will lengthen thy days.

And Solomon awoke; and, behold, it was a dream. And he came to Jerusalem, and stood before the ark of the covenant of the LORD, and offered up burnt offerings, and offered peace offerings, and made a feast to all his servants.

99. Solomon Dedicated the Temple

2 Chronicles 6:12-42 KJV

And he stood before the altar of the LORD in the presence of all the congregation of Israel, and spread forth his hands: For Solomon had made a brasen scaffold of five cubits long, and five cubits broad, and three cubits high, and had set it in the midst of the court: and upon it he stood, and kneeled down upon his knees before all the congregation of Israel … said, O LORD God of Israel, there is no God like thee in the heaven, nor in the earth; which keepest covenant, and shewest mercy unto thy servants, that walk before thee with all their hearts: Thou which hast kept with thy servant David my father that which thou hast promised him; and spakest with thy mouth, and hast fulfilled it with thine hand, as it is this day.

Now therefore, O LORD God of Israel, keep with thy servant David my father that which thou hast promised him, saying, There shall not fail thee a man in my sight to sit upon the throne of Israel; yet so that thy children take heed to their way to walk in my law, as thou hast walked before me ... let thy word be verified, which thou hast spoken unto thy servant David.

But will God in very deed dwell with men on the earth? behold, heaven and the heaven of heavens cannot contain thee; how much less this house which I have built!

Have respect therefore to the prayer of thy servant, and to his supplication, O LORD my God, to hearken unto the cry and the prayer which thy servant prayeth before thee: That thine eyes may be open upon this house day and night, upon the place whereof thou hast said that thou wouldest put thy name there; to hearken unto the prayer which thy servant prayeth toward this place.

Hearken therefore unto the supplications of thy servant, and of thy people Israel, which they shall make toward this place: hear thou from thy dwelling place, even from heaven; and when thou hearest, forgive. If a man sin against his neighbour, and an oath be laid upon him to make him swear, and the oath come before thine altar in this house; Then hear thou from heaven, and do, and judge thy servants, by requiting the wicked, by recompensing his way upon his own head; and by justifying the righteous, by giving him according to his righteousness.

And if thy people Israel be put to the worse before the enemy, because they have sinned against thee; and shall return and confess thy name, and pray and make supplication before thee in this house; Then hear thou from the heavens, and forgive the sin of thy people Israel, and bring them again unto the land which thou gavest to them and to their fathers. When the heaven is shut up, and there is no rain, because they have sinned against thee; yet if they pray toward this place, and confess thy name, and turn from their sin, when thou dost afflict them; Then hear thou from heaven, and forgive the sin of thy servants, and of thy people Israel, when thou hast taught them the good way, wherein they should walk; and send rain upon thy land, which thou hast given unto thy people for an inheritance.

If there be dearth in the land, if there be pestilence, if there be blasting, or mildew, locusts, or caterpillers; if their enemies besiege them in the cities of their land; whatsoever sore or whatsoever sickness there be:

Then what prayer or what supplication soever shall be made of any man, or of all thy people Israel, when every one shall know his own sore and his own grief, and shall spread forth his hands in this house: Then hear thou from heaven thy dwelling place, and forgive, and render unto every man according unto all his ways, whose heart thou knowest; (for thou only knowest the hearts of the children of men:)

That they may fear thee, to walk in thy ways, so long as they live in the land which thou gavest unto our fathers. Moreover concerning the stranger, which is not of thy people Israel, but is come from a far country for thy great name's sake, and thy mighty hand, and thy stretched out arm; if they come and pray in this house;

Then hear thou from the heavens, even from thy dwelling place, and do according to all that the stranger calleth to thee for; that all people of the earth may know thy name, and fear thee, as doth thy people Israel, and may know that this house which I have built is called by thy name.

If thy people go out to war against their enemies by the way that thou shalt send them, and they pray unto thee toward this city which thou hast chosen, and the house which I have built for thy name; Then hear thou from the heavens their prayer and their supplication, and maintain their cause. If they sin against thee, (for there is no man which sinneth not,) and thou be angry with them, and deliver them over before their enemies, and they carry them away captives unto a land far off or near;

Yet if they bethink themselves in the land whither they are carried captive, and turn and pray unto thee in the land of their captivity, saying, We have sinned, we have done amiss, and have dealt wickedly;

If they return to thee with all their heart and with all their soul in the land of their captivity, whither they have carried them captives, and pray toward their land, which thou gavest unto their fathers, and toward the city which thou hast chosen, and toward the house which I have built for thy name:

Then hear thou from the heavens, even from thy dwelling place, their prayer and their supplications, and maintain their cause, and forgive thy people which have sinned against thee. Now, my God, let, I beseech thee, thine eyes be open, and let thine ears be attent unto the prayer that is made in this place.

Now therefore arise, O LORD God, into thy resting place, thou, and the ark of thy strength: let thy priests, O LORD God, be clothed with salvation, and let thy saints rejoice in goodness. O LORD God, turn not away the face of thine anointed: remember the mercies of David thy servant.

100. Stephen Prayed for His Murderers

Acts 6:8-12 NIV

Now Stephen, a man full of God's grace and power, did great wonders and miraculous signs among the people. Opposition arose, however, from members of the Synagogue of the Freedmen (as it was called)—Jews of Cyrene and Alexandria as well as the provinces of Cilicia and Asia. These men began to argue with Stephen, but they could not stand up against his wisdom or the Spirit by whom he spoke.

Then they secretly persuaded some men to say, "We have heard Stephen speak words of blasphemy against Moses and against God."

So they stirred up the people and the elders and the teachers of the law.

Acts 7:51-60 NLT

"You stiff-necked people, with uncircumcised hearts and ears! You are just like your fathers: You always resist the Holy Spirit! Was there ever a prophet your fathers did not persecute? They even killed those who predicted the coming of the Righteous One. And now you have betrayed and murdered him— you who have received the law that was put into effect through angels but have not obeyed it."

When they heard this, they were furious and gnashed their teeth at him. But Stephen, full of the Holy Spirit, looked up to heaven and saw the glory of God, and Jesus standing at the right hand of God. "Look," he said, "I see heaven open and the Son of Man standing at the right hand of God."

At this they covered their ears and, yelling at the top of their voices, they all rushed at him, dragged him out of the city and began to stone him. Meanwhile, the witnesses laid their clothes at the feet of a young man named Saul.

While they were stoning him, Stephen prayed, "Lord Jesus, receive my spirit." Then he fell on his knees and cried out, "Lord, do not hold this sin against them." When he had said this, he fell asleep.

101. The Prayers of All the Saints

Revelation 8:1-6 NIV

When he opened the seventh seal, there was silence in heaven for about half an hour.

And I saw the seven angels who stand before God, and to them were given seven trumpets.

Another angel, who had a golden censer, came and stood at the altar. He was given much incense to offer, with the prayers of all the saints, on the golden altar before the throne. The smoke of the incense, together with the prayers of the saints, went up before God from the angel's hand. Then the angel took the censer, filled it with fire from the altar, and hurled it on the earth; and there came peals of thunder, rumblings, flashes of lightning and an earthquake.

Then the seven angels who had the seven trumpets prepared to sound them.

Do You Have a Relationship With God?

The Bible tells us that:

> *... if you confess with your mouth, "Jesus is Lord," and believe in your heart that God raised him from the dead, you will be saved.*

Romans 10:9 KJV

HAVE YOU ACCEPTED JESUS AS YOUR LORD?

If you do not have a relationship with God – through accepting Jesus as Lord – then I invite you to please pray the following prayer:

Lord, I come before you today to confess that I accept Jesus as my Lord and Savior and that I believe you raised Him from the dead. I believe that He died for my sins and that only through Him can I be saved.

Lord, please forgive me of all my sins and accept me into your Kingdom. Lord, I welcome the Holy Spirit into my heart today.

I thank you, Lord, in Jesus' Name, Amen.

Congratulations! Now, you - as a born-again Christian can best maintain your walk with God by:

- Praying daily – ask God to help you with the challenges in your life and to bring you closer to Himself
- Read and Study God's Word (the Bible) daily
- Attend a Bible teaching church
- Fellowship with other serious Christians

A good place to start your Bible reading is with the book of John.

If you have questions or need help please write to me at:

Akili Kumasi
GOD IS LOVE MINISTRIES
P.O. Box 80275, Brooklyn, NY 11208
kumasi@GILpublications.com

Mail Order ....GIL Publications
P. O. Box 80275, Brooklyn, NY 11208
Telephone Orders...............(718) 386-6434
Website Orders ....www.GILpublications.com

SCRIPTURE REFERENCE BOOKS			
Book Title	Price	#	Total
God's Healing Scriptures 240 Prayers & Promises in the Bible	$9.95		
101 Women in the Bible	$6.95		
101 Prayers in the Bible	$6.95		
101 Victories in the Bible	$6.95		
HALL OF FAITH CLASSICS			
Volume 1: The Person and Work of the Holy Spirit (R.A. Torrey)	$9.75		
Volume 2: How to Pray (R.A. Torrey)	$5.95		
Volume 3: How To Obtain the Fullness of Power for Life and Christian Service (R.A. Torrey)	$5.75		
Volume 4: Absolute Surrender (Andrew Murray)	$6.25		
Volume 5: Humility: The Beauty of Holiness (Andrew Murray)	$5.75		
Hall of Faith 5-Pack (Volumes 1, 2, 3, 4, 5) - $25% off – Save $8.35	$25.10		
FATHERHOOD BOOKS			
Fatherhood Principles of Joseph the Carpenter	$8.95		
Fun Meals for Fathers and Sons	$4.95		
On the Outside Looking In	$7.95		

To pay by Credit / Debit Card – go to www.GILpublications.com or call 718-386-6434

Complete the Order Form on the next page

Mail Order .... GIL Publications
P. O. Box 80275, Brooklyn, NY 11208
Telephone Orders .... (718) 386-6434
Website Orders .... www.GILpublications.com

Book Title	Price	#	Total
Bible Word Search – Puzzles with Scriptures (80 puzzles per book)			
Vol. I: **Extracts** from the Bible	$7.95		
Vol. II: **Women** in the Bible	$7.95		
Vol. III: **Fathers** in the Bible	$7.95		
Vol. IV: **Prayers** in the Bible	$7.95		
Vol. V: **Victories** in the Bible	$7.95		
Vol. VI: **Parables** in the Bible	$7.95		
Vol. VII: **Promises** in the Bible	$7.95		
Vol. VIII: **Foundations** in Christianity (100 Puzzles)	$8.95		
Bible Word Search 8-Pack (all 8 books) - *17% off – Save $11.00*	$53.62		
Bible Word Search, **Large Print, No. 1**	$5.95		
Church Edition CD - *560 puzzles –* (7 volumes, lesson plans, group activities)	$5.95		
Eᴅᴜᴄᴀᴛᴏʀ's Wᴏʀᴅ Sᴇᴀʀᴄʜ Vol. 1: U.S. Presidents	$5.95		
Sub-Total			
NY Residents Add 8.5% Tax			
Shipping ($3.95 1st item, 50¢ each additional)			
TOTAL			

Date:_____ Payment: ▣ Check ▣ Money Order
Name:_____
Address:_____
City:_____ State:_____ Zip:_____
Telephone:_____
E-Mail:_____

www.ingramcontent.com/pod-product-compliance
Lightning Source LLC
Chambersburg PA
CBHW061729020426

42331CB00006B/1156